❸ LIGHT CAMPING ❸

ith almost daily change of camp sites. *Constraints:*
ery limited means of resupply and help in trans-
ort; weight and bulk. *Examples:* husky wilderness
ikers and canoeists with light canoes.

*smaller variety of foods. Eliminate: canned
stove, Dutch oven.*

T ❷

eans of resupply, and with
oes or small boats; light
o Use This Book."

*ate: beans, some rice and some flour, canned
stove, Dutch oven, reflector, and grill. Add:
ry foods.*

❹ VERY LIGHT CAMPING ❹

ith lightest possible and most compact supplies
d gear. *Constraints:* no means of resupply; weight
d bulk; time for cooking; no interest in camping
s such. *Examples:* hikers who must carry heavy
ulky gear for special uses such as photographers.

THE CAMPERS' COOKBOOK

THE
CAMPERS' COOKBOOK

Equipment
Recipes
Menus

By
LUCY G. RAUP

CHARLES E. TUTTLE COMPANY
Rutland, Vermont

Representatives
Continental Europe: BOXERBOOKS, INC., Zurich
British Isles: PRENTICE-HALL INTERNATIONAL, INC., London
Australasia: PAUL FLESCH & CO., PTY. LTD., Melbourne
Canada: HURTIG PUBLISHERS, Edmonton

Published by the Charles E. Tuttle Company, Inc.
of Rutland, Vermont & Tokyo, Japan
with editorial offices at
Suido 1-chome, 2-6, Bunkyo-ku, Tokyo, Japan

Book Plan by Roland A. Mulhauser
Library of Congress Catalog Card No. 67-15139
International Standard Book No. 0-8048-0079-0
PRINTED IN JAPAN

To
H. M. R.

TABLE OF CONTENTS

Part I: Getting Ready to Cook

Part II: Actual Cooking

FOREWORD
By Dr. E. M. GOULD

TODAY WHEN MORE OF US than ever before live in crowded urban areas, outdoor recreation is an ever increasing leaven for city life. This trend seems likely to continue.

This is also a time when peoples' taste for camping is changing rapidly, and often the first experience living out of doors will determine whether the family ever goes again. A week of rain the first time out may dampen more than clothes, blankets, and enjoyment.

Reading this book can't change the weather, but it can give the camper an important edge that can change the memory of a trip from folly to fun. Satisfying food can make a vital difference on a trip to the woods, lake, or ocean. Equally important is the need to suit the food and equipment to the parties' capacity to comfortably move it from place to place.

Too many neophytes fail to realize that as trips away from resupply points get longer and transportation becomes muscle power that the proper kind of grub assumes a central note. Carrying too heavy a pack can spoil an otherwise perfect trip. Even when cars, canoes, or horses are available to do the hard work, having the right food and preparing it with a minimum of waste effort is central to a pleasant trip.

This is the first book I have seen designed to help ease the way from one kind of camping to another. I hope it will be widely used so that more and more people will find pleasure in getting away from city life and moving easily in our great outdoor spaces.

Editor's note: **Dr. E. M. Gould,** well-known in the field of recreational planning, is a forest economist on the staff of the Harvard Forest at Petersham, Massachusetts, which is a part of Harvard University. He is much interested in the multiple use of forest lands and has been working on problems dealing with the recreational uses of these lands.

Preface
WHY A CAMPERS' COOKBOOK

THERE ARE NOW millions of people who spend part of each year camping, and the number is increasing rapidly. Some go for overnight; some for more or less regular weekends; and others for longer periods.

The kinds of camping these people do is extremely varied. Some timid souls may be sleeping out and cooking away from their home kitchens or backyards for the first time ever; others may have done a great deal of camping of one particular sort and are now trying another kind entirely new to them. They may be doing trailer camping after having gone always to a fixed site which has been taken for granted as a second home; others may be taking a plunge into wilderness camping, with canoe or pack train. All too frequently these adventurous souls run into difficulty with planning their equipment, or with their food and its preparation.

It is true that our basic needs, food, clothing, and shelter, are the same whether we are at home or camping out. However, the satisfying of these needs is greatly influenced by environment. The same food, the same clothing and the same sort of shelter do not fit all situations. What could be sillier and more disasterous than no hiking boots in rough mountainous country, or frozen food and no way to keep it frozen. To be sure these are extreme cases of people taking the wrong kind of clothing and supplies, but such things do happen. The poor man with the sandals had to wait until some one sent him proper foot-gear before he could climb the mountain. The frozen food had to be eaten when it thawed, not a few days later as was planned. Just as sad and discouraging is too much and too elaborate equipment and food. And strange as it may seem, equipment and supplies can be too simple. Wilderness cookbooks have a way of saying: "Travel light, reduce everything to a minimum. Use lard pails for cooking pots." This is all very well, but what does one do with the lard while he cooks on the first part of the trip? Put it in his pocket?

Why a campers' cookbook? Why not use the old favorite from the home kitchen? This would be fine if one has the appurtenances of the home kitchen: stove, refrigerator, freezer, and supermarket. But then one is not camping! The very word *camping* implies that it is a more or less temporary and different way of living. By the same token, *camp cooking* is a simplified and specialized form of cooking. Everything changes when one goes camping—the stove, the food, the appetites of the people, and sometimes even the cook! Most home cookbooks fit the campers' needs no better than home or city clothing. We leave these things behind so we must leave our home cookbooks behind as well.

Because the kinds of camping are now so varied, their effects upon camp cooking are likewise varied and complex. In cabin or cottage-living there is usually a simple stove which may or may not have an oven. In established camp sites where there is trailer or tent space there are likely to be fireplaces with fuel provided. For a more nomadic form of camp life, now commonly called "wilderness camping," an entirely different approach is needed. The stove or fireplace must be made of the things at hand, perhaps rocks, logs, or even banks of sand. It can be seen readily that each of these

— 14 —

kinds of camping as well as many others calls for special equipment, and sets up special restrictions on the cooking gear and the food carried. Thus it would seem that a great deal of thought and planning make the basis of good camping and good camp cooking.

Sometimes camp cookbooks are put together by reassembling gleanings from other cookbooks. They are compilations. Others have their beginnings in basic home cooking tried out in camp and the results appraised. Successful methods and recipes are kept and the failures discarded. This little book has evolved by the second method.

Voluminous notes were kept on twenty-odd camping trips ranging in length from over-night to two- and three-month journeys in the Canadian North. The means of travel covered the gamut of possibilities, from walking with a pack to modern air transport. The number of people to be planned for, sheltered, and fed varied from two to fourteen. Complete and careful estimates of supplies and equipment were made before each trip and then notes on the suitability of these things were kept during the journey. Changes in recipes and the new ones developed were recorded at the time, commonly with menus and the supplies used in them. At the end of each trip an inventory was made and used to revise the gear and grub lists for the next trip.

Notes of this kind are useful as data from which to make a camp cookbook. But anyone who cooks knows that they are lifeless without the addition of personal skills and something that has to be called "flair." Only this can transform the raw data into a genuine campers' cookbook. The author of this book has always *liked* to cook, especially in camp. Her product, if it achieves its purpose owes much to this, and a great deal also to the very real, though often intangible, results of camping and cooking under the direction (usually quite unconscious on their part) of Masters of the Art. There have been several of these—men for whom camping had almost lost its status as a temporary way of living. Vivid is the memory of Dave Watson stopping within sight of "home" and cooking dinner over an open fire although "home" boasted no mosquitoes or blackflies and a stove with oven. Time determined dinner, not kitchen facilities. Then there was Frank Dent, whose breakfasts of flapjacks, perfectly shaped and browned, set his standard of excellence. No one ever produced a good cooking fire more quickly than Oliver, a Cree Indian. He taught his skills by quietly doing. These men and many others are in the pages of this little book, though their names may not appear.

These notes plus a knowledge of home cooking have been the basic material going into this Campers' Cookbook. It has seemed sensible to merge the two extremes, basic home cooking techniques and those of wilderness camp cooking, into a book which encompasses the material needed by campers of any sort in any of the usual situations. This is a departure from the pattern by which camp cookbooks have been written. Over the last fifty years there have been cookbooks written for campers but they have always dealt with one or at the most only a few kinds of camp cooking. This necessitated consulting a different book when the kind of camping changed—a most inconvenient procedure.

This little book approaches the matter in a different way. It has two parts—first, Getting Ready to Cook, and second, Actual Cooking. Both parts are planned to cover a wide variety of kinds of cooking. There are ways of doing things, pieces of equipment and recipes which are equally usable in many situations and some that are peculiar to only a few.

HOW TO USE THIS BOOK

MOST COOKBOOKS DEVOTE practically all of their pages to recipes and more recipes. That is not the case with this book. The recipes are here, better than 200 of them, but there is also space given to the consideration of kitchens and provisions. The reason for this may not be immediately obvious. Cookbooks are usually written for one set of conditions— the same kitchen, the same provisions, and the same means of resupply. In the case of a cookbook for campers of more than one kind, as this is, all these things change. Sometimes the production of good meals becomes easier as the constraints imposed by weight and means of resupply are eased. In other cases, these limiting factors become more restricting and are augmented by other constraints such as the bulk of provisions and the experience of the camper. All these factors and many more are reflected first in the ration list.

Information and ideas about provisioning and ration list building, some general and some specific, are found in Chapter Three. Raup's Basic Ration List, given on page 64, is the one from which all other lists are derived. A new list suitable for campers with other constraints than those operating on this basic list can be arrived at by simple additions and subtractions in the master list. This makes for flexibility and gives room for the exercise of personal choice on the part of the camper.

Using this system of making additions to or subtractions

from her Basic Camp Ration List, the author separates the different kinds of camping into five distinct catagories and shows how a camper can go from one kind to another, unknown to him, with ease and confidence. Pertinent information applicable to each of these five kinds of camping are marked throughout the text with the following symbols:
❶ ❷ ❸ ❹ ❺

❶ Camping at permanent sites where the replenishing of supplies is not a serious problem and where the weight and bulk of the supplies and equipment are not important, as for example cabin or auto-trailer camping. In this instance Raup's Basic Camp Ration List, page 64, can be augmented with a greater variety of foods, more canned goods and some fresh, a stove and a refrigerator.

❷ Camping at frequently changing sites where one has some aid in transport, but limited opportunity to replenish supplies, as for example on trips with large canoes, small boats, light aircraft, or pack animals. This is the kind of camping for which the Basic Ration List is designed.

❸ Camping at constantly changing sites where one has very limited access to transportation or means of resupply, and where weight and bulk are important factors, as for example while hiking in a wilderness or traveling by small canoe. For this kind of camping one must eliminate from the Ration List all canned foods and do without a portable stove and Dutch oven.

❹ Very light camping where weight and bulk are vitally important, where one has no means of replenishing supplies, and possibly no interest in or time for camp cooking, for example while hiking and having to carry heavy bulky gear for special purposes other than camping itself. Not only should one refrain from taking canned goods, a portable stove, reflector, grill, and Dutch oven when doing this kind of camping, but should also eliminate beans and reduce the amount of rice and flour. Freeze-dry foods, on the other hand, are very practical under these conditions.

❺ The lightest kind of camping possible, on short trips during which one has no means of replenishing supplies and is very limited in camping and cooking experience, as for example beginners and light hikers, young families, older persons, Boy and Girl Scouts. All uncooked and canned foods should be eliminated from the Ration List, no stove, Dutch oven, reflector, or grill should be carried, and most of the cooking pots should be replaced with heavy aluminum foil pans. Freeze-dry foods in meal units or their equivalent are especially recommended.

Chapter One
CAMP KITCHENS

THE PLACE WHERE food is to be prepared merits some consideration in camp as well as at home. If a person is building a new house a great deal of time and money are spent in planning and equipping the kitchen or cooking area. Sometimes, even, a specialist is called in just to design that part of the house. This procedure, of course, would be absurd in setting up a camp kitchen, but a bit of careful planning should be done.

In planning a camp kitchen the first thing to do is set aside a portion of the living space, whatever that may be, for the use of the camp cook. This can be quite simple. It is a plan of living that has evolved through the centuries since man first learned to change the form of his wild food by cooking. Primitive peoples, whether nomadic or those living in permanent shelters, set aside special areas for specific uses. The Eskimo has his sleeping shelf, while his cooking lamp or stove is in a separate place. The tent Indian has his cooking fire outside the tent, or if it is in the tent it is in a fixed spot and there is a certain place for food. Simple huts or cabins are so arranged that the food is stored and prepared in a special place. In any camp it works well to follow the same plan. Otherwise there probably will be some sort of disaster, such as the "green" camp cook had when he took his tightly closed sourdough pot to bed with him—it exploded and made a horrible mess.

If the camper is using a cabin or trailer the kitchen area is already planned and the space set aside. It can be quite compact and yet complete. In such a setting, order and cleanliness are all that are needed to make a good kitchen. ❶

In a trailer camp equipped with fireplaces the campers often prefer to use the cooking facilities in the trailer. Or if the trailer is not so equipped they prefer to use a small portable stove for most of their cooking and use the fireplace as a source of heat and cheer around which they sit in the evenings. The only cooking done at the fireplace may be the late evening pot of coffee or cocoa. Essentially the same system may be followed in wilderness camps—a small fire is used for cooking in a special fireplace and a larger fire is made for warmth and cheer. There may even be another small smoke-producing fire for smudging insects. At first glance all these fires might seem a waste of fuel and a poor use of space and time, but actually they often make good sense. A large fire produces too much heat for most cooking, while a smudge makes an unsatisfactory cooking fire and a most uncomfortable and unhappy cook.

Whether the camp is in a cabin, a trailer or in the shelter of a spruce tree, the basic characteristics of orderliness and cleanliness are of first importance. An example comes to mind. A small group of people was established in a tent camp which was to be used for two months. Some time and effort had been spent making a comfortable, handy camp. A good cooking fireplace had been built of rocks and located in such a way that it was convenient. A rick of firewood was near at hand and so stacked that it could be easily covered to protect it from rain; the cooking pots were hanging near the food preparation center; a dining-work table had been made of poles and sheltered from sun and rain by a tarpaulin stretched over a frame of poles; food supplies were either in closed boxes at the end of the table or on a cache so built that it had good protection from bears. This, all in all, was a beautiful, orderly but very simple camp kitchen. Then what happened? Visitors came with the most elaborate equipment of every sort. By bedtime that evening the camp was a shambles. The fireplace rocks had been removed to make seats around the cooking fire. The cooking fire had become the center of a story-telling group and the cook could not get near without asking someone to move. An open can of coffee was sitting on a stump halfway between the "cupboard" and the fireplace; dishes, either clean or dirty were just where someone had lost interest in them; gadgets workable and otherwise, sleeping bags and clothing were strewn everywhere. All in all everything was ready to give the squirrels, chipmunks, and porcupines such a night of revelling as they had never had. A rain in the night was the only thing needed to make the next day the kind to make the most dedicated camper tempted to give up and go home.

This sort of happening must be avoided and it can be. The kitchen area must be kept intact for its assigned purpose. If we plan an orderly kitchen we will have three areas—food preparation, cooking, and storage. Each of these spaces may be quite small, as in a trailer, but this is not a disadvantage if they are kept neat and clean.

Perhaps one of the largest problems in setting up a camp kitchen is to keep from making it too complicated and too well equipped. It is best to start with a minimum of equipment and then add only the things really needed. A camp kitchen is no place to store or care for things which are used only rarely. The care of the kitchen should not become a burden.

KITCHEN EQUIPMENT

In a book of this size there is not space to discuss all the things available for a camp kitchen. We shall consider briefly the most usable pieces of equipment and let the reader browse through the camp outfitters stores and catalogs for other items which seem to fit his special needs. Most "real" campers like to select their own equipment. They may even like to make some pieces which they are convinced are far better than those available in the stores. This is part of the fun of camping. Camp gear is the topic of many evenings talk around campfires.

Stationary Stoves. Most trailers and hired cabins come equipped with some sort of cookstove. These usually use electricity, "bottled" gas, or oil for fuel. Because they are so common it may be assumed that anyone camping can operate them. If the cabin or trailer does happen to have no cookstove one may be chosen from a wide variety. Either a compact trailer stove or the usual home kitchen stove may be used if size is right. 🔵

Wood-burning stoves are often found in cabins which are away from electric lines and not on access roads suitable for the delivery of gas or oil. These stoves are excellent if in good repair (grates and oven). However, it does take a little practice before one learns to operate such a stove efficiently. If the camper has a choice of wood burners he should try to get one with both oven and hot water reservoir. The addition of these two items will do much for the efficiency and flexibility of the cooking unit.

The proper use of the dampers in a wood-burning stove determines whether it works well or not. There are usually three dampers. One is located at the base of the firebox under the grate, and partially controls the fire (draft). The second is in the stove pipe and also helps determine the rate at which the wood burns. The third usually is located at the back of the top cooking surface and either sends the heat around the oven before it goes up the chimney or causes it to go directly out the chimney. It determines whether both the oven and the top of the stove are heated or only the top of the stove. The two draft-dampers, the one under the firebox and the one in the stove pipe, must be open until the fire gets a good start. The fire is built as is any wood fire—see section on wood fires page 37. The damper controlling the heating of the oven is best closed at this time. When the fire is burning well, both the draft-dampers should be partly closed. If the oven is to be used, its damper should be opened and the oven preheated before cooking in it is started. Most beginners keep too big a fire. This only wastes fuel and makes both the top of the stove and the oven too hot for cooking. Also it needlessly heats up the kitchen.

If the stove has no oven one can be added in a section of the stove pipe, or a portable oven can be used on the top of the stove. The stove pipe oven is merely a box-like enlargement of one section of the stove pipe. It is a bit primitive but quite flexible when one has learned to use it. It should be placed in the stove pipe about three feet above the firebox. Such ovens are most easily found in northern outfitting stores which supply hunters and trappers in northern Canada and Alaska.

Another source of supply for compact camp stoves is the small boat outfitter. One small "boat" stove is made of soapstone and burns charcoal. It is rather intriguing and might be good for a cabin, especially if the cooking stove is also used as a space heater. The soapstone holds heat much longer than the thin sheet metal which is used in most camp stoves. ❶ ❷

Portable Stoves. Never has there been such a wide selection of light weight stoves as is now available. If one explores the field the proper stove to fit any need from very light weight ones for hiking trips to heavier ones suitable for tent kitchens or even trailer or cabin use can be found. ❷ ❸ ❹

The types of fuel used are just as varied—alcohol (liquid and solidified), kerosene, gasoline, butane gas, charcoal, wood, and coal. One word of caution—gasoline which is a very popular fuel with campers is highly explosive. It should be handled with utmost care and only by experienced people. Even then it is extremely dangerous. Eskimos and travelers in the North have had many tragedies from exploding gasoline stoves. It is much wiser in most cases to use kerosene even though the fire is harder to start and produces more soot.

The simplest "stove" for very light cooking is a can of solidified alcohol—"Sterno" by trade name. A burning match is all that is needed to start it and the heat is intense. The alcohol is not affected by low temperatures and will not spill. Light weight folding stoves using this fuel are available, some one-burner and some two-burner. They can be found in most hardware stores. An improvised stove may be made by placing the can of Sterno on the ground between two logs or rocks upon which the cooking pot is placed. A wind screen can be made by cutting the ends out of a large tin can and punching some holes near the bottom of the resulting cylinder. The holes improve the draft and the cylinder concentrates the heat in addition to protecting the flame from too much wind. The bottomless can is slipped over the can of alcohol and the cooking pot placed above it. A Seven-ounce can of Sterno will burn for about two hours. It must be remembered though that this is a small heater and cannot be expected to heat a large kettle quickly. It is best for tea-making, warming a bit of precooked food, or very light cooking. ⑤

The Swedish Primus stove has been popular with Arctic travelers and mountain-climbers for many years. It burns kerosene under pressure, produces intense heat and is capable of cooking large amounts of food quickly. It does have drawbacks and will probably be replaced by some of the butane gas stoves. Primus stoves are notoriously hard to start and hard to keep going. They require frequent filling and pumping if the pressure is to be kept up. If the flame goes out, the hot stove is likely to be difficult to start. If a Primus stove has a large full kettle on it, it is top heavy and there is real danger of an accident from a spilled kettle. Such a kettle should be taken off the stove when the stove is being pumped up.

There are many other one-and two-burner kerosene or gasoline stoves on the market and many of them are much safer and less trouble to use than the Primus. Some of them are quite compact—folding into suitcase-like carrying cases.

Another type of portable stove burns artificial gas. There are several of these available in various sizes. Fuel is carried in disposable cans or cartridges. An adequate supply of fuel should be taken for the stove being used since it may be hard to find the proper fuel in a container which fits the stove in question.

One of the several wood-burning stoves on the market probably is preferable if the camper is going to a region where he can get firewood easily. In this case he carries only the stove and not both the stove and the fuel. Some of these stoves fold and are quite compact and light in weight. It may take a little time shopping, before the most suitable one is found. Wood-burning stoves are often used on long trips with pack-animals. They may have either built-in or portable ovens. Most wood-burning stoves can also be used for burning charcoal or briquettes.

There is room here to describe in some detail only one such stove. It is called the "Raemco 7 in 1." In one small package, no larger than $10'' \times 21'' \times 12''$ plus a folding oven, $10'' \times 15'' \times 12''$, and weighing no more than 44 lbs, cormes the most complete and versatile camp stove the writer has seen. It is completely portable, and is suitable for use outdoors, in a tent, or in a cabin where it may be set up permanently. It is made of substantial sheet metal and burns wood, coal, charcoal, or briquettes. It broils, smokecooks, barbecues (rotisseries), fries, bakes, stews, and roasts.
It will hold a fire, if properly banked, for several hours. There are a number of accessories which may be had. The only thing that would add greatly to its usefulness is a hot water reservoir. In a fixed camp two stoves, one for cooking, and the other fitted with a water tank on top or at the side would be excellent. ❶ ❷

Grills. A common piece of backyard cooking equipment, the grill, in one form or another, may find a use in the camp kitchen. It is commonly used for broiling but its usefulness need not stop there. It is just as handy for any top of stove cooking. Most outdoor cooks are familiar with grills. Department stores, hardware stores, as well as camp outfitters carry a variety of them. The more elaborate ones are best suited to backyard or patio cooking. ❶

Fireplaces. By fireplaces is meant both indoor and outdoor "working" fireplaces. An indoor cooking fireplace can be considered a luxury and rightly so. However, if the cabin is to be used in late fall or winter, such a fireplace can be fun. It can be a simple orthodox fireplace or one of the modern "package" kind. Either one, equipped with a crane, trivets, or grates (there are some swinging ones made just for indoor fireplaces) and a dutch-oven or a reflector oven, with or without a spit, is equal to any demand made on it. If one is building a cabin for winter use, a cooking fireplace might be included. It offers recreational possibilities when the weather is bad, and it might appeal especially to Scouts or older people. ❶

Outdoor fireplaces can be as varied as the imaginations of their builders. We are all familiar with the assortment of backyard and patio creations so popular at the moment. There is neither space nor need to discuss them here. A few guide lines for building cooking fireplaces will be more useful. The design will be left to the imagination of the builder.

The word fireplace suggests not just a *place* for a fire but rather a partially enclosed place. There is good reason for the enclosure—the heat of the fire is more concentrated, fuel lasts longer, smoke is carried away better and there is somewhat less danger of the fire getting out of control.

Permanent Fireplaces. Actually the word permanent is not good. What is meant is a fireplace which is used many times on many different occasions. Its repeated use gives reason to spend time and material on it. ❶ ❷

The materials used in constructing a camp fireplace are varied but it is best to use the materials at hand whether rocks, sand, loam, or logs. Such fireplaces fit the landscape and are more fun to build and use.

Stone fireplaces, if made of the stones of the area, are especially fitting and at the same time efficient. First the vegetation and humus layer of the soil are removed (this is good fire control practice) in a space 3 by 4 feet. If large flat rocks or small roundish ones are available this space may be paved with them. If such stones are not available the floor of the fireplace may be covered with gravel, sand, or loam. Then a stone wall is built around three sides of this rectangular space leaving one long side facing the prevailing winds open. The end walls may be from 8 to 12 inches high but the long wall, back of the fireplace, should be higher—18 to 24 inches. This high side acts as a reflector of the heat and is especially useful if a reflector oven is to be used. One or two stones at the base of this wall should be removable. Their removal will greatly improve a poor draft.

Green logs about six inches in diameter, preferably of slow burning wood, may be used instead of rocks to build the walls. Two stakes about two or three inches in diameter are sharpened at one end. These stakes are driven in the ground just behind the bottom log of the long wall, one near each end. They should slant a little away from the fire. The green logs are laid one on top of the other against these stakes until the "wall" is of the desired height. Walls made of logs will have to be watched to prevent them from becoming a part of the cooking fire as they become dry. If they are kept slightly damp, they will last longer. If they do begin to burn while the fire is being used for cooking, a few cups of water can be poured over them without doing much damage to the cooking fire. When the logs are too dry for use as reflectors, they can be used for firewood and replaced by fresh green ones.

A fireplace can be made with ridges or banks of soil or sand in place of rocks or logs. It will not be as good looking but will serve quite well. Sometimes wind will blow the sand a bit and if there is danger of its being blown into the food the banks may have to be dampened; or if one has plenty of aluminum foil it may be spread over the walls to keep them in place.

Temporary Fireplaces. Fireplaces to be used just a few times can, of course, be built in the same way as the ones just described, or aluminum foil supported by wooden stakes may take the place of more lasting wind brakes and heat reflectors. ❷

Kettle Supports. There are any number of ways to support kettles over a campfire—some simple and others more elaborate. A few of the common and satisfactory types will be considered here.

Camp Grates. Although camp grates have certain limitations —they always get warped or bent, are hard to put up on rocky ground and are always black with soot when they have to be packed—they are convenient for many uses. They may be had either with or without legs. If without legs, the grate is rested on rocks or logs. The most satisfactory fire under a grate is a criss-cross one in which split wood is used. A grate cannot be used over a high baking fire. It is best to pull some of the coals out to one side of the fireplace and keep a small fire going under the grate. ❷ ❸ ❹ ❺

Crane. Several pots are much more satisfactorily managed if they are hung above the fire. A crane is the most satisfactory way to do this. For a crane select two forked stakes about 1½ to 2 inches in diameter and about 3 to 4 feet long, and a long straight pole, about 5 feet long, of about the same siz·ə Sharpen the ends of the two forked sticks and drive them firmly into the ground about four feet apart with the forks parallel with the ends of the fire. Place the third stick across the forks. Sticks with perfect forks are not found very often, so be satisfied with fairly regular ones. ❷ ❸ ❹ ❺

A less artistic but quicker and even more satisfactory way to get "forked" stakes is to make them. Select four stakes about 1 to 1½ inches in diameter and about 3 to 4 feet long. Drive two of these into the ground at each end of the four-foot fire space. The two stakes should be about 10–12 inches apart at the ground and driven at a slight angle so the tops may be pulled together, crossed and tied to produce the fork in which the cross-pole, or lug-pole rests.

The kettles are hung from the cross-pole (lug-pole) by pot-hooks of varying lengths. Chain pot-hooks may be bought at outfitting stores, or hooks may be made in camp from no. 8 wire, or made from crotches of green branches. Cut the larger side of the crotch longer and notch it for the kettle bail on the *inside* near the end. Several pot-hooks of varying lengths are convenient to adjust the kettles over the fire for varying heat. The pot-hooks need not be thrown away when camp is moved but may be taken along, thus saving time at the next place.

Logs or Fire-irons. Perhaps the simplest method of supporting kettles over a fire is to place two green logs about 8 inches in diameter and about 3 or 4 feet long side by side but closer together at one end than at the other. The kettles are then placed on these logs suiting the diameter of the kettles to the space between the logs. The same result may be obtained by using stones or fire-irons instead of logs. Fire-irons are two pieces of *flat steel* approximately 3 feet by 1 inch by ¼ inch. ❹ ❺

Slanting Poles. One or even two kettles may be quickly and quite satisfactorily supported on a pole slanting over the fire. This is accomplished by sticking one end of a pole, possibly 6 or 8 feet long, in the ground or under rocks and resting it on a forked stick, log or more rocks in such a way that a kettle hung from the other end is at the desired height above the fire. Notches for the bails of the kettles should be cut at the end over the fire. These notches keep the kettles from sliding down the pole. ❹ ❺

Tripod Support. For cooking with only one pot a tripod placed over the fire is satisfactory. The distance of the kettle above the fire can be changed by moving the tripod legs closer or farther away from the fire. The poles should be wired or tied together with string at the top. The kettle is hung by string, wire, or chain.

COOKING FIRES

Appetizing camp meals of well-cooked foods are dependent not only upon raw food materials of good quality but also to a great extent upon the way they are cooked. This, in turn, depends largely upon the suitability of the fire over which the food is cooked. The most juicy steak can be quickly and thoroughly ruined either by an extremely hot fire which burns it to a crisp or by a slow fire which permits it to stew. Likewise, the most excellent bread or cake can easily be ruined by the wrong kind of fire.

Wood Fires. The prerequisite, and perhaps most important requirement for a good cooking fire is plenty of good dry wood of suitable size. The writer's experience has been largely limited to northern regions and as a result she feels competent to cite woods of that region only. For a more detailed and broader discussion of firewoods the reader is referred to *Camping and Woodcraft* by Kephart (see Bibliography). In a general way, it may be said that hardwoods such as hickory and maple are to be preferred to softwoods if they are available, and that dry, dead, or at least seasoned wood, is to be preferred to freshly cut green wood. Among the northern woods spruce (Picea glauca), lodge pole pine (P. contorta) and jack pine (Pinus Banksiana) are of first choice. These are followed by birch (Betula papyrifera) and balsam popular (Populus Tacamahacca) and aspen (P. tremuloides.)

The bark of the birch makes excellent kindling which will start a fire under almost any conditions. It is a splendid idea to have a small reserve supply of birch bark in a dry place to be used in extremely wet weather. It does, however, produce a tremendous amount of dense smoke and deposits a thick layer of soot on the cooking pots. The bark of large old balsam poplars makes a very hot quick steady fire with little smoke. It can be gotten either from trunks of down trees (care should be taken to procure only dry bark) or it may be knocked from the standing trees. The bark, however, produces a relatively large amount of ash. Well-seasoned tamarack makes a fairly good fire wood. Willow and alder can be used with little success except when a small amount of actual cooking is to be done, such as for lunches. Willow is very poor, being hard to keep going and producing a large amount of ash. Alder is somewhat better in that it produces a hotter fire but burns out very quickly. Willow and alder

— 34 —

are useful though, when a quick hot fire is needed for a few minutes only. There is an advantage, too, in that the twigs may be broken by hand without the use of an ax.

There are two general types of fires: one to be used for several meals and for cooking that requires considerable time, and one to be used for a single quick meal. The general method of building them is the same but it varies some in detail.

Before actually starting to build any fire, whether it is to be used to cook one meal or many, there are a few things to be considered and done. First, the place where the fire is to be located must be considered carefully. A place convenient to water, wood, and near to the place where the food is kept is essential. All inflammable material should be cleared from a space twice as big as the proposed fire is to occupy. If the grass is dry or if there is a drought or windy weather the top soil should be completely removed. These precautions may seem unnecessary for just a lunch fire, but a puff of wind can cause even a small one to get out of hand.

After the location for the fire has been selected, gather kindling. This kindling may be dry birch bark, dry dead pine needles or the small dry dead twigs from the lower dead branches of trees. No twigs should be taken from the ground because these are almost certain to be damp. Then collect a supply (armful) of slightly larger sticks and a good supply of larger wood, preferably from a dead standing tree which has been chopped into convenient lengths and then split.

To start the fire, pile the birch bark or the pine needles loosely in a little mound—do not pack them down tightly. In the absence of either of these shave three or four small dry sticks almost through for about half their length. Stand them up in the form of a pyramid with the shaved ends down.

Carefully lay on more small sticks and strike a match to the kindling. As the fire burns, carefully and slowly add more sticks and increasingly larger ones until fairly large ones are being used and the fire is burning well. If the fire is to be used just as a quick one for one meal it is ready to use. If it is to be used for many meals a little more work may profitably be spent on it. (See Fireplaces, page 29.)

An Indian system of placing small saplings on the fire, the tips radiating from the fire like the spokes in a wheel may be used. As the fire burns down move the sticks in toward the fire. This method does save a great deal of chopping and also is useful if the fuel supply is low. However, it is not a very satisfactory fire for any other than the simplest of cooking.

Charcoal and Briquette Fires. As every backyard cook knows charcoal and briquettes make excellent cooking fires. Real charcoal makes a quicker fire but does not give as intense or long lasting heat as briquettes. It is a little better for quick cooking, and briquettes are perhaps a bit better for rotisserie cooking. Some cooks like the fragrance of charcoal better than that of briquettes. ●

Fires using these fuels are sometimes hard to get started. The usual method is to use kindling, or one of the many fire lighters on the market. Either charcoal or briquettes must burn a few minutes to a half hour before they are right for cooking anything. The charcoal or briquettes are burned down to coals with white ash beginning to appear before the heat is correct. Most beginners use too much of the fuels and make too large fires. This is expensive and makes the fires unsatisfactory for cooking. Patience and practice are necessary in learning to handle these fuels. If the cooking is finished before the fuel is consumed, it may be wetted down and added to the next fire.

Fires for Baking. Baking fires require more care and different types of baking equipment require different sorts of fires.

Frying-pan Baking. Frying pan baking requires the simplest fire. Almost any good fire which is fairly high and at the same time has some coals is quite satisfactory. ❷ ❸ ❹

Reflector Baking. The reflector works best with a high fire built in front of a good reflector wall.

Dutch-oven Baking. Coals are essential for producing good results with a Dutch oven. If the available wood supply is such that there is difficulty in getting plenty of coals one of the other methods of baking should be chosen. ❷

A large fire of hardwood, either green or dry, will quickly produce a good supply of coals if it has a good draft. Also the thick bark of hardwoods such as poplars produces good coals. If it is desirable to keep the coals a while they may be covered with ashes.

HOT WATER SUPPLY

If the camp does not have a stove with a reservoir a bit more thought will have to be given to the supplying of hot water. If a large topped stove is used a big kettle or teakettle can be kept at the back where it will receive some heat. It may be "moved up," when convenient, to be heated more. ❶

In a camp where a fireplace is used either for cooking or

pleasure, a large metal container filled with water (5 gallon is a good size) can stand at the edge of the fire. It will produce a fair supply of hot water without taking up space over the cooking fire. A small fire will keep such a kettle hot. ❷

EXTINGUISHING CAMPFIRES

If wood or charcoal is used in fireplaces or open fires in camp, nothing is more important for a camper than the habit of always putting old campfires out very thoroughly. This is best done by drenching them with water (*buckets* and *buckets of water*) or by smothering them with dirt or sand. It is well to see that any roots under the place where the fire is to be built are cut and torn out. Fires have been known to travel by burning along such roots. ❷ ❸ ❹ ❺

KITCHEN UTENSILS

Camp outfitters must be extremely conservative. The design of cooking kits has changed very little over the last fifty years. The same good points and the same poor ones are still in most sets, so be prepared to modify the one you buy. Most units are designed for four persons.

Basic Aluminum Cook Kit—4 persons, total weight approximately 5¼ lbs.
   1 7–8 qt. kettle with cover and bail
   1 4–5 qt. kettle with cover and bail
   1 2–3 qt. kettle with cover and bail
   1 6–8 cup coffee pot
   1 9½ in. frying pan with detachable or folding handle
   1 7½ in. frying pan with detachable or folding handle
   4 8¾ in. plates

4 cups

1 carrying case

These changes make a much more flexible kit:

1. Replace coffeepot with a small (2 qt.) kettle of same kind as the other kettles so it will nest inside them. It can be used for coffee as well as for other cooking. The coffeepot in these ready-made units is too small and the spout is a nuisance—it won't pour and is hard to keep clean.

2. Replace the aluminum frying pans with sheet steel or copper bottomed ones. Be sure the handles on the replacements either fold or are detachable. Aluminum frying pans are light in weight but do not cook well—they burn the grease but do not brown the food properly. Food sticks to them.

3. If the cups are aluminum replace them with enamel or plastic. The edges of the aluminum ones become too hot.

4. Add 2 plates for serving.

5. Add heavy 4 mil polyethylene bags to hold the kettles for packing. If the kettles have been used over smoky fires they are too sooty to pack one inside another.

6. Add a flat-bottomed straight-sided aluminum pan large enough to fit over the bottom of the largest kettle. This pan serves as a mixing bowl, dish pan, casserole and many other utensils.

7. Be sure the carrying case is durable—waterproof canvas or nylon, and large enough to take the revised kit.

This basic kit has a certain amount of flexibility. As it comes it can be used for parties of 3 to 6 persons by simply adding or subtracting plates and cups. For much smaller or larger groups it is well to change the sizes of kettles.

There is a very beautiful set made by the Revere Copper and Brass Co. It is especially suited to boat or trailer camping. It is not suitable for open wood or charcoal fires because of the kind of handles used. It does not include plates or cups. ❶ ❷

Cutlery and Silver. The most common camp "silver" is stainless steel. There is a wide selection to choose from. A basic set consists of:

4 forks
4 soup or dessert spoons
4 knives—may be dispensed with if all campers carry pocketknives and do not eat in the European manner!
2 large spoons for cooking and serving
1 butcher knife—only if much fresh meat is to be used. Hunters have their own pet knives for butchering.
1 paring knife—only if fresh vegetables are to be used.
1 French chef's knife
1 small steel or knife sharpener
1 cloth roll carrying case for cutlery—may be bought from outfitters or made at home.

Dutch Oven. A heavy iron or steel pot with bail and sunken-topped cover is considered indispensable by many veteran campers. When one learns to use it, fine cake, bread, stews, and roasts may be produced. ❷

Reflector Oven. Excellent and much lighter in weight than a Dutch oven. It can produce equally good baked food. Its operation is more easily mastered because the food in it is visible at all times. It does require more fuel than the Dutch oven. ❷ ❸ ❹

The reflector oven is nothing more than two slanting pieces of aluminum or tin which reflect the heat from a fire in front of them upon a pan midway between them. The ends are closed and all pieces are hinged together so that when not in use the reflector may be folded. There are two types of reflectors, one with a single joint at the back and the other with two. The one with two joints gives the baking pan a little more room, which is sometimes an advantage, but the other is more compact.

A canvas carrying case is a great convenience. It is well to have it made with three compartments or pockets, the center and largest one for the reflector, one side pocket for the baking pan, and the other for the cooking grid.

The baking pan is best made of dark steel, because it absorbs rather than reflects heat. When the pan is new there may be some difficulty in keeping it from rusting. A light greasing with a bacon rind is effective.

To secure best results with a reflector, it must be bright and shiny, so it is well to carry a small cake of bon-ami or mild scouring powder. Lava soap does very well, is compact and easily carried.

Pressure Cooker. This might be considered a gadget. If the weight is not of too great importance a pressure cooker is a fine addition to the cooking outfit. There is a light weight one on the market. It is made of stainless steel, holds two quarts and weighs about 2¼ pounds. ❷ ❸

A pressure cooker has many advantages. Foods are cooked much more quickly in it than by any other means, tough meats can often be made tenderer. A pressure cooker is almost indispensable for high altitude cooking. It is ideal for the preparation of dehydrated foods. Cooking pressure actually accelerates rehydration of dried foods. And last but not least, a great deal of fuel is saved because the cooking time is so much reduced.

If a pressure kettle is to be carried be sure to include the cookbook and instruction sheets that come with it. Follow the directions carefully.

Gadgets. There are a few miscellaneous items that are needed in any kitchen. They are usually things which appeal to the individual cook but some are common to most cooks.

CANISTERS. These need not be metal but if they are offer best protection against gnawing animals. Plastic containers or even waterproof cloth bags may serve the purpose. If plastic bags are used they should be made of heavy 3 mil polyethylene plastic. Whatever the material, the containers should be of various sizes to hold the staples in constant use such as flour, sugar, salt, pepper, shortenings, and seasonings, as well as a few leftovers.

SPATULA.

MEASURING CUP AND MEASURING SPOONS. These may be an ordinary cup and spoon of the camp equipment that have been calibrated and marked by comparing them with the home measures.

SMALL 1- OR 2-MAN COOKING OUTFIT. Either a Boy Scout or "Placo" cooking kit is very handy for hiking trips away from the base camp. Children especially enjoy a lunch on the trail if they have possibilities for cooking it. ❸ ❹ ❺

CAN OPENER. Take your favorite type if it is not electric.

ALUMINUM FOIL. Heavy duty foil serves many purposes in a camp kitchen. Food may be wrapped in it for storage, or for cooking over or in the fire. Improvised cooking utensils may be made of it on short trips when you must travel light. One company has produced disposable foil frying pans. Some of the foil pans for freezer use would serve for this, especially if wire racks or handles are improvised.

Water Containers

JEEP OR JERRY CANS. Since the war these cans have been widely used for carrying or storing the camp's water supply. They are compact, durable, close tightly, pour reasonably well, and the five gallon one holds as much as a person wants to carry. If metal cans are chosen care should be taken to get those free from rust. The original war product for water storage had an enamel lining. Plastic containers made like the metal ones are now available. ❶ ❷ ❸ ❹

CANVAS BUCKETS. These are good for hiking or other trips where bulk and weight are important factors. The "canoe model" which has an easily closed inner throat piece is preferable. ❷ ❸ ❹

STORAGE

Cabin and Trailer. The amount of space needed for food storage is not very great in most camps. Trailers and cabins will, most likely, have shelves and cupboards for such use. If a large quantity of food is to be stored in a cabin for a long time, a small room or walk-in closet is useful. This unit must provide protection against mice, rats, squirrels, and other animals. Metal boxes or screen-enclosed shelves serve best. ❶

Caches. In wilderness camps where mice and squirrels are joined by porcupines and possibly bears, real care must be taken to protect the food supply. A system that has proven satisfactory in the north consists of building a platform, or small cabin built on a platform, high above the ground. To make this "cache" three or four trees, 10 or more inches in diameter and the desired distance apart, are selected. They are cut off about 12–14 feet above the ground and any branches removed from the resulting stumps. A firm platform of poles or poles and boards is built on top of the stumps. The tree stumps must have wide bands of tin tightly fastened to them several feet above the ground to prevent animals, such as porcupines, from climbing up and getting to the food. Some trappers fasten huge fish hooks to the posts with the sharp points down to make climbing more difficult. Care must be taken to make it impossible for squirrels to jump from nearby trees to the platform—there must be no trees near enough! ❶ ❷

If the food is piled on the platform and not in a "cabin" it must be carefully covered with waterproof canvas in such a way that rain will drain off and not run under or into the food. The canvas must be lashed down to keep the wind from carrying it away.

If the cache is to be a permanent installation it is well to build a small house on the platform. This may be made of poles and have a sod roof or it may be of any more elaborate building material available.

Access to the cache is by ladder. This ladder must always be removed when not in use—animals can climb up it if it is left in place.

Camp Pantry. No matter what kind of camping is to be done

there are a number of staples and odds and ends that are needed frequently, if not for every meal. These things are best kept as a unit and not packed with general supplies. One company makes a box for them which it calls a "Camper's Kitchen." It is a simple plywood box with quickly assembled legs. One side of the box is hinged and drops down to become a work table. The inside has compartments of various sizes.

A fine pantry could be made of fiber panniers opening on the wide side instead of at the top which is the usual way. A set of compartments could be inserted if desired. The usual size of panniers $(22'' \times 9'' \times 17'')$ would be excellent. Two such cases would be adaptable for any except back-packing trips.

For hiking trips where the supplies are much reduced a small fiber box could be used in the same way. ❷

The larger outfitters especially those catering to trips with pack animals can supply or have these pantries made up to special order. Traveling salesman's sample cases can be adapted to the same use.

Cool Storage. In a good many situations cool storage is important. Trailers or cabins supplied with electricity or gas present no problem. Either standard or smaller sized portable refrigerators can be used. ❸ ❹

There are many portable ice refrigerators or cold boxes on the market. The best of these is the simple box without gadgets. It may be made of plastic or double metal boxes with an insulating layer between them. Whichever one you choose should have a tight fitting cover, and you should test its keeping qualities at home! Such a box is cooled with a chunk of ice (a big chunk melts less rapidly than cubes and is more compact). Heavy 3 mil polyethylene bags are good food containers for these boxes. ❶ ❷

Coleman makes a nice "station wagon" box. In the top is a plastic container for ice. As the ice melts the resulting water may be drawn off by a faucet and used for drinking. The space below the ice is used for food storage. This box opens on the side.

If camp is made beside a stream or spring, food may be kept cool by partially submerging a box or can in the water. The problem here is to anchor the box or can so that it will not be carried away by the constant tugging of the flow of the water. ❶ ❷ ❸ ❹

Garbage Disposal. Garbage draws flies and animals, even bears. Good public camp grounds provide a means of garbage disposal but it can become a real problem in the private camp. Some campers burn it but seldom is it dry enough to burn without leaving a wet partly-burned mess. A better system is to bury it, or burn and bury. A trench, at least 2 feet deep, should be dug at some little distance from the camp. It should be large enough to hold several days' refuse. It is good practice to pour some sort of disinfectant over the garbage frequently. This keeps flies and odor at a minimum. After a reasonable accumulation, the amount depends upon the climate, a layer of dirt is shoveled over the garbage. A fire may be built in the trench and as much of the garbage as possible is burned before it is buried. Tin cans should be burned out and flattened before they are put in the pit for burying. Dishwater and other kitchen liquid wastes should be poured in the garbage trench, not thrown promiscuously around the camp. All garbage pits should be thoroughly covered with dirt and made as inconspicuous as possible before camp is moved!

Protection from Flies. It is amazing how fast flies, especially blowflies, find a new camp. They seem to arrive with the camper. They are just as adept at finding perishable foods, especially ham, fresh meat, and fish. Actually they can lay their eggs on ham while the cook is cutting a slice or two. They are not much attracted to bacon.

In a permanent camp, without refrigeration, a tight screen box is a good container for perishables. Large lengths or large bags of fine-meshed nylon netting (bridal veiling in the trade) do extremely well in other camps. Care must be taken that the netting does not touch the food or it may be contaminated by a fly sitting on the outside.

Chapter Two
PROVISIONS:
SELECTION AND PACKING

SELECTION

There was a time when the selection of foods suitable for
camping trips was difficult because of the absence of many
light-weight nourishing foods. In order to cut back on
weight and bulk, the grub list was reduced until most of the
time it sustained life but in a monotonous manner. The only
hope of the camper was to supplement with wild fruits, fish,
and game. Today's camper, the one for whom this book is
written, has less opportunity for "finding" food than did his
earlier counterpart, but he can select from an almost bewil-
dering array of suitable foods. The problem, now, is to keep
from taking such a variety that his camp meals become one
long parade of tasting bees. That, too, can be monotonous.

There was a time when camping was almost entirely *wilderness* camping—hiking, canoeing, or hunting trips with
pack animals. These were clean-cut trips. When one actually
sallied forth on such a trip he left all semblance of home living
behind. Today, there are many kinds of camping and one
moves readily from one kind to another. One day he may be
living rather elaborately in cabin or trailer and the next off
on the trail with his kitchen and pantry on his back. It is the
ease with which the camper makes this transition that determines his pleasure in the whole undertaking and there is no

better place to prepare for this change than in the provision list.

There are four forms of food from which the camper may choose— fresh, canned, simple dehydrated, and freeze-dry. Of course, there is no hard and fast rule that one kind can be used for only one kind of camping, but the keeping qualities, weight, and bulk do influence the choice.

Some fresh vegetables are much more adapted to camp use than others. As a rule root vegetables, potatoes, onions, carrots, and turnips are the most durable. They are compact with a minimum of loss in preparation and they keep well. They, with the addition of cabbage which keeps almost as well, form the basic fresh vegetables for camp use. Leafy vegetables are most perishable and can be kept for only short times if unrefrigerated. They do supply vitamins but under camping conditions these are better supplied by canned or dehydrated vegetables.

Another drawback to fresh vegetables is their high water content. Leafy vegetables, such as spinach, are as much as 88% water; potatoes are 50% water.

Fresh meat, fish, and poultry are even more perishable than vegetables and fruits. Depending upon the temperature they will last only a short time without refrigeration—not more than a day or two in warm weather. Pork, veal, poultry, fish, hamburger and organs, such as liver, should be cooked within a day if the weather is warm and humid.

Fresh fruits, except apples and citrus, are all perishable and have too high a water content and too great a bulk to make them good basic camp foods.

When fresh foods are no longer practical we turn to canned ones. They are fine; we like their flavor; and if available and can be transported, they solve, for most camping, the problem of keeping food without refrigeration. However, they still present problems of bulk and weight—they are even heavier and bulkier than fresh foods because the weight of the water and sometimes sugar plus the weight of the container have been added to that of the original food.

Dehydrated products go much farther toward supplying the camper with foods low in bulk and weight. The naturally dried ones, if they may be so classified, beans, peas, lentils, rice, and grains have become, through ages of use, accepted as good although they vary greatly from their fresh counterparts. The early camper's grubstake was made up largely of them— beans, bacon, and bannock. Then through the years we have added dried fruits—dates, figs, prunes, apples, and a few home dried vegetables and meats such as corn, dried beef, "jerky" and pemmican. The present generation of campers will accept all of these, with the possible exceptions of jerky and pemmican, as good, forgetting that they taste very different from the fresh.

For many years a great deal of experimentation has been carried on in an effort to produce good dehydrated foods which still have a pleasing texture and flavor. The early attempts were discouraging but the last few years have brought some good results. The older and better-known form of dehydrated food is produced by using dry heat to extract the water. The texture and taste of the food changes in the process. Only lean meat may be treated this way because the fat becomes rancid. However, some of these products are good and if carefully selected and treated are truly satisfactory.

A recent development has been a new process combining freezing and dehydration. It is still somewhat in the experimental stage but gives great promise of light weight, nourishing, and pleasing foods. At present only a few of these foods have found their way to our grocers' shelves— mushrooms, some flaked potatoes, sauces, soups, and coffee (not instant). Most outfitters and suppliers, however, are now stocking a wide variety of these freeze-dry foods. One catalog carries a list of 96 individual items and 12 complete dinners as well as several main dishes. Most of these products are excellent; their flavor and texture are much superior to the earlier dehydrated products. They are quite acceptable if treated as the directions instruct. However, they can be improved if a bit of extra attention is given to their seasoning. The instructions are clear and concise. In fact, anyone who can read and take direction can produce excellent meals.

A great deal of attention has been given to make the packaging attractive to campers. It is durable, light in weight and in some cases can be used as cooking utensils.

Freeze-dry foods are admirably suited to the needs of special campers—the young, Scouts, even Cubs and Brownies, those who must travel light, and older campers who no longer wish to be bothered with heavy rations.

A few words of warning should be given about the use of freeze-dry foods, however. So far the products of the several companies are by no means standardized. Some are excellent while others are too poor to bother with. Do try them before buying for a camping trip. The appearance of meat has not been improved but its lack of attractiveness is more than compensated for by the flavor and variety it brings to the camp table. The portions as sold by most processors are too small. The cost is high but, many times, the savings gained by reduction in weight and bulk more than conpensate.

Meats and Fish. Fresh meat and fish are the first choice.

BACON AND HAM. Select those with heavy country cure. Most ordinary cures such as those on super-market counters keep the meat for only a short time without its becoming rancid. If it is to be kept without refrigeration for an extended time it is better to choose tinned cured products.

FISH. Smoked or smoked and dried fish, which keep better, make good camp foods.

CANNED MEATS AND FISH. Solid packs without gravy or sauce are to be preferred. One gets tired of always having meat served in the same gravy. Fish packed in oil is better than that put up in brine. The oil can be used in cooking.

DEHYDRATED OR FREEZE-DRY. Meats are available in greater variety than seafood. Shrimp and crab treated in this manner are excellent.

DRIED BEEF. This is an exellent food. If used in quantity, buy it in a solid chunk—not sliced. It may be hard to find in this form. There is a packer in Texas who puts up an excellent smoke-dried beef. He sells by mail order. See page 189.

SAUSAGES. The hard salamis are good for snacks and lunches.

Eggs. Be sure to buy freeze-dry eggs if fresh ones are impractical. Beware of both egg substitute (baking powder does as well) and dried eggs made by the early air-dry method.

Milk. Use either powdered or evaporated milk for general use. There is a condensed form but it is too sweet for most uses and is not as convenient.

Butter. Canned butter cannot be differentiated from fresh. Buy 1–1b tins. The butter keeps no better than fresh after the tin has been opened.

Cheese. Cheese is an old stand-by in camp. It is a good form of concentrated protein. Buy large chunks, not slices, because it keeps better. Cut edges may be greased and the cheese wrapped in aluminum foil or the chunk may be wrapped in a cloth saturated with diluted vinegar before being enclosed in foil.

Breadstuffs. Rycrisp, flatbröd, pilot's bread (ship's biscuit or hardtack) are convenient substitutes for baker's bread. They go farther and are more durable than the usual crackers. There are several tinned breads on the market but most of them are not very palatable. Many of the tinned ones have been too well fortified with all the things that are "good for us." Sometimes toasting a tinned bread will improve it a little. An exception to the rule is New England brown bread. It cans well.

Cereals. Quick cooking brown cereals are best for camp use. They are compact, cook easily and supply a little of the roughage that is lacking in many camp diets. Instant cereals (freeze-dry) can be had.

Flour. White, unbleached, is more pleasing to most people than whole wheat or rye flours. If the darker, heavier flours are used, carry a little white to use with them, in pastry and for thickening soups and stews. Cornmeal, either white or yellow, is good for part of the supply. It is good as a cereal, for coating fish and for making bread.

Leavening Agents. BAKING POWDER: Use double action. It goes twice as far. BAKING SODA: Baking soda improves some kinds of sour dough baking. It is used in some quick breads and has medicinal uses. GRANULATED DRY YEAST: Be sure to check the expiration date that is stamped on the package. Granulated is the best form in which to carry yeast. It is light in weight and keeps about a year. A package of this yeast if added to a sour dough starter will hasten its action.

Sweet—Sours. The novice is likely to under-estimate the value of these.

SUGAR. The bulk of the supply should be granulated. A little brown is handy for seasoning and for making syrup. Include extra sugar for the first two weeks of a wilderness trip.

JAMS—JELLIES. These are important in a camp diet. Some of the freeze-dry spreads are good. Honey is an excellent camp sweet. It can be had in a granulated form that is easier to carry than the more usual liquid form.

CHOCOLATE. Hershey is making a "Tropical Bar" that is semisweet, slow melting and fortified with vitamin B1. Try it. Milk chocolate has a low melting point and is a nuisance on some trips. Be wary of some of the chocolate energy bars—they are heavily fortified and concentrated which makes them best for strenuous wilderness trips.

PICKLES—SAUCES. A little of these can do a great deal toward making a taste change. Chutney is especially welcome and its use is not confined to curry. It is fresh-tasting and interesting but it is so concentrated that a little goes a long way.

Vegetables. Dehydrated and freeze-dry vegetables enormously improve camp diets with little additional weight and bulk. A few ounces of chives, onions, green peppers, and parsley will do wonders for many dishes. Other vegetables give variety, vitamins, and minerals. Use the kinds packaged separately; then they can be used mixed or unmixed as desired. Tomato paste, if used with a light hand, will impart a tomato flavor to many things besides spaghetti. It can be air or oven dried and used later dissolved in water.

Fruits. Pack various kinds of dehydrated fruits separately. They can then be used straight or mixed as fits the occasion.

Fats and Oils. Vegetable fats and oils keep longer without becoming rancid than do animal fats. Solid fats are much easier to transport and store than liquid ones. Margarine keeps longer than butter. Bacon fat, especially if care is taken to keep it from burning, is excellent for cooking, even pies can be made with it. If much bacon is used the camp has an ever renewing supply of fat. Never throw it away! Woodsmen in the north use bacon fat in place of butter on bread as the Danes use drippings from roast pork.

Beverages. To the basic coffee, tea, cocoa, and milk, consider adding some of the concentrated fruit juices. Try them at home first, though, because many are insipid, overly sweet, and no improvement upon water or lemonade (made from concentrate).

Maxwell House has put out a freeze-dry coffee that tastes more like fresh coffee than does instant coffee.

Condiments. An example: beef may be served "au naturel" one time, curried another, and seasoned with chili peppers still another time. Such use of condiments does much for a plain diet.

Curry powder, chili powder, lemon concentrate (in the plastic "lemon"), and your own special ones are worth having in the grub-box.

Snacks. These are hard to find in the usual camp kitchen unless they receive special attention when the ration list is being made. Chocolate, raisins, dates, figs, hard candies, malted milk, malted-milk tablets, cheese and sardines—all are essential to a happy camp.

PACKING

The mass of food for a camping trip is always much larger than seems reasonable and the packing of it a mountainous task. Great loss of time, comfort, and even food can result from poor packing.

If the trip is to be longer than a week or two it helps to do the shopping and packing in units of supplies for units of time. Most outfitters will pack provisions in units as the buyer desires. This saves the camper a tremendous amount of time in sorting and repacking. Sometimes there is a small charge for this service. The writer, for long trips, has the grub packed in unit lots, each covering two weeks for the whole party, plus one lot of miscellaneous items, mostly seasonings and small luxuries, which are hard to divide. ❷ ❸ ❹

Sometimes it is practical to have each person's rations packed separately and for specific units of time. This is only advisable if the party is on a strenuous trip and together less time than separated. It does not contribute anything to the general morale and gemütlichkeit of the group. It seldom fits a party camping for pure pleasure. ❹

Packing in individual lots can be a nuisance. The writer remembers one trip when she fell heir to the cooking. There was a motley lot of travelers on board a tug and barge—Indians, trappers, government personnel, scientists, and adventurers, twenty-five in all. Each individual or small group had his own grub supply. There was one small stove in the tiny galley. Shortly before meal time the keeper of each larder presented the cook with his food so that she might take from it his share for that meal. A bit had to be taken out of each ration or for some time to come its owner might be short of a basic item, possibly bacon, sugar or coffee. The only thing that made this form of cooking and feeding at all possible was the similarity in the supplies—mostly beans, bacon, and bannock.

The units of supplies can be packed in boxes made of cardboard, wood, or fiber. Cardboard is light in weight and quite satisfactory unless it is likely to get wet in transport or storage. Wood is excellent but heavy and expensive. Fiber is light weight and can be durable. These individual containers should not be heavier than one person can move or if to be carried by pack animal not heavier than 75–80 pounds. (Burros can carry somewhat heavier loads than horses.) ❷ ❸ ❹

If one is interested in having more or less permanent, light weight containers, fiber boxes or telescopes are a good investment. Some outfitters have such cases, usually called "fiber box panniers," or they can be made to order by sample case manufacturers. The best are made of strong fiber, the corners reinforced with leather or metal, and they are closed by strong leather or web straps. Their tops are telescoping so there can be some adjustment in size. A practical size is $22'' \times 9'' \times 17''$. This size packs well in a station wagon or car trunk. It is the right size for a side pack on a pack animal and holds a reasonable amount. About the only kind of transport to which panniers are not suited is by small canoes (they pack well in freight canoes) or back packing. Even then a man can carry one over a portage. It is convenient to have one or two panniers opening on the $17'' \times 22''$ side; the rest should open on the $22'' \times 9''$ top.

Fiber panniers must be kept well varnished and protected from excessive damp, otherwise they will warp. With reasonable care, they will give years of service.

For those times when bags are more suitable than boxes most outfitters have duffel bags of waterproof canvas. Cheaply made, light weight ones are not worth buying— they tear easily and are not waterproof. The best are made of 13-oz. waterproof duck with reinforced handles riveted on, and with an inside waterproof throat-piece which, when tied, prevents dust, dirt, and water from entering. Duffel bags are not as convenient to use for food as fiber boxes but on some trips they are essential. Don't get them too small; such are a real aggravation. A good size is $18'' \times 36''$ or even $21'' \times 36''$. ❷ ❸

There is a wide assortment of containers for individual items—boxes, bottles, and bags. The best of these are made of metal, plastic, or waterproof cloth. These come in a wide variety of shapes and sizes. Plastic bags should be made of a heavy grade and well sealed. Some outfitters sell flat-bottomed bags made of paraffined cotton duck for food storage. They are most durable, stand up well on their flat bottoms and impart no flavor or odor to their contents. A roll or several sheets of heavy plastic is useful for some packaging.

Chapter Three
RATION LISTS AND MENUS

SOMETIMES THE QUESTION of rations and menus is tossed off lightly by the writers of camp cookbooks with such comments—"A grub list seldom suits anyone except the compiler; let the camper make his own." There is more than a grain of truth in this but why not offer a few guide lines that may be helpful to the person doing the planning? They might keep someone from arriving in camp only to find that he has no salt or that he has lots of syrup for pancakes but no baking powder for making them.

There are various ways to go about making a ration list. Here is a way which will produce one that is truly yours and whether it will be satisfactory or not will depend upon your accuracy. By this method you start with a blank piece of paper and list upon it every bite of food, and its weight, you use in a given length of time. If the food is not used as it comes from the market, all the ingredients called for in its preparation must be included, even salt and pepper. The resulting list will be appalling in its length, variety, and total weight. At best, you will have only a record of what you ate within a given time. It will vary somewhat from a list made at a different time. This list must be revised before it can be used on a camping trip. Certain unsuitable items must be taken out and replacements made with other better adapted choices. To make a grub list by this method is a terrific job.

A second way to work out a ration list is to make a set of menus covering every meal and every snack for the proposed camping trip. Then compile a list of the foods used in these menus. The resulting list becomes the ration list. This method, like the one above, involves a huge amount of labor, and will only be good for one particular trip. However, it may be worthwhile to use this method if there are special dietary problems.

A third way to arrive at a grub list is to use one of the basic lists given in some book on camping. Perhaps your tastes are just like those of the author of the book; and, if so, all is very simple. More often there are differences that must be taken into consideration. If the basic list calls for oatmeal and if you don't like oatmeal, you better change the list! Don't just leave it out or your total cereal supply will be short by that much. Again, if you are so fond of oatmeal that you want a double portion or want it twice a day, you must change the list accordingly. So it goes, each item on the list must be scrutinized before the shopping is done and the trip in progress.

Here are several lists which have been developed for different situations.

TRAILER AND CABIN RATIONS ①

Food selection for a camp in a trailer or cabin, equipped with a refrigerator and with easy access to market, needs no special ration list. Marketing will follow the same pattern as that used by the camper at home. However, there should be a well-stocked emergency shelf. It should have upon it the makings of several good quick meals, and a few easily assembled meals for impromptu trips away from the base camp. An emergency shelf is stocked mostly with canned and freeze-dry foods. Here is a suggested list and it may be adjusted to suit the needs of the individual.

EMERGENCY SHELF LIST

Salt
Pepper
Butter—tinned
Shortening
Sugar
Flour
Tea
Instant coffee
Milk—powdered
Bacon—canned
Ham—canned
Fish—canned
Rice

Vegetables-canned or freeze-dry
Bread-stuffs—brown bread, flatbröd
    crackers
Hot bread mix
Pancake mix
Soups—freeze-dry
Chocolate—semisweet
Malted milk
Fruit—canned or dehydrated
Assorted freeze-dry meals
    „   „   „ main dishes
Baby foods (?)

BASIC RATION GROCERY LIST ❷

4 persons/2 weeks; approximate weight 5 lbs/person/day.

Tea	1 1b.
Coffee	5 1b.
Chocolate or cocoa	1 1b.
Fresh bread	6 lge. loaves
Flour	40 1bs.
Biscuit flour	assorted
Buckwheat flour	to suit
Yellow corn meal	customer
Rice	5 1bs.
Rolled oats	3 1bs.
Macaroni	2 1–lb. pkgs.
Baking powder	3 8–oz. tins
Yeast—granulated	4 envelopes
Canned vegetables	12 no. 2 tins
Canned baked beans	6 no. 3 tins
Canned potatoes	24 no. 2 tins
or fresh potatoes	30 lbs. (½ bu.)
Canned onions	6 no. 2 tins
or fresh onions	6 lbs.
Other fresh vegetables	6 lbs.
Canned fruits	8 no. 2½ tins
Raisins, seedless	4 1–lb. pkgs.
Evaporated fruits	5 lbs.
Prunes	3 lbs.
Salt pork	10 lbs.
Bacon	15 lbs.
Ham	1 (14–15 lbs.)
Dried beef	3 9–oz. jars

Canned meats	4 lbs. net
Canned fish	4 lbs. net
Codfish, boneless	1 3–lb. box
Soup, canned	6 sml. tins
Soup, freeze-dry	6 pkgs.
Eggs	4 doz.
Butter in tins	6 lbs.
Peanut butter	1 12–oz. jar
Cheese	2 lbs.
Crisco	3 lbs.
Canned milk	28 sml. tins
or milk powder	3 1-lb. tins
Sugar	10 lbs.
Syrup, maple	½ gal. tin
Jam, jelly, and marmalade	5 lbs.
Olives	2 pt. jars
Salt	2 2–lb. pkgs.
Pepper	¼ lb. tin
Worcestershire sauce	1 sml. bottle
Vegetable oils	1 sml. tin or bot.
Tomato ketchup	1 bot.
Mustard	1 sml. tin or bot.
Vinegar	1 16–oz. bot.
Mayonnaise	1 sml. bot.

This list was made up from items on any grocer's shelves. It has been used as a basic list when dehydrated or freeze-dry foods were not wanted or available. It was expected that it would be supplemented by game or fish.

When a two-week's supply of food for four persons is assembled by this list, it makes a mountainous stack. The average daily weight of 5 to 5 and ¾ pounds per person is too much to be transported or stored easily.

RAUP'S BASIC CAMP RATION LIST: ❷

4 persons/2 weeks; approximate weight 2 ¾ lbs./person/day.

Flour (white)	35 lbs.	
Cornmeal	3 „	
Sugar—granulated	12 „	
Sugar—brown	1 „	
Cereal, quick cooking	8 „	
Bacon—tinned	18 „	
Corned beef—tinned	5 „	
Ham—tinned	14 „	
Rice	4 „	
Beans—white pea	5 „	
Prunes	5 „	
Dried peaches	5 „	
Cheese	4 „	
Salt	2 „	
Raisins	2 „	
Chocolate	3 „	
Butter—tinned	4 „	
Jam—tinned	4 „	
Milk—powdered	4 „	
Coffee—vacuum packed	3 „	
Tea	1 „	
Cocoa		8 oz.
Tomatoes—2 no. 2 ½ tins	3 „	
Dehydrated vegetables		
Beans—green	1 „	8 „
Potatoes—raw sliced	2 „	
Potatoes—cooked flakes	2 „	
Onions		8 „

Carrots	1	lbs.		
Cabbage	1	„		
Julienne	1	„	8	oz.
Spinach			8	„
Squash (hubbard)	1	„	8	„
Beets	1	„		
Corn	2	„	8	„
Freeze-dry soups—assorted	2	„		
Soup-bases, chicken & beef			8	„
Miscellaneous small items				
Pepper			2	„
Baking soda			4	„
Baking powder			7	„
Dry mustard			4	„
Cinnamon			4	„
Cornstarch			4	„
Vinegar			8	„
Mustard pickle			8	„
Chutney			8	„
Bran—all			8	„
Crisco			8	„

Emergency cache

Sugar	Amounts depend upon time
Flour	involved, ease of transporta-
Rice	tion, and nearness of supply
Salt	point.
Tea	
Baking powder	
Bacon (tinned)	

This list has resulted from the constant revision of lists of many trips. It has been used on pack horse, canoe and light aircraft trips without change; and it has been reduced for hiking trips and expanded when there was easy transport by truck.

As it stands this ration list has proven to be generous and with leeway enough to take care of an occasional guest in a group of young adult campers. Amounts of coffee, tea, and cocoa are too small to supply a regular late evening pot in addition to use at meals. The supply of materials for lunches should be increased if more than light lunches are wanted. Bacon grease must be saved for use in cooking, even baking. Greater variety of meats could be given by replacing some of the bacon, ham, and corned beef with freeze-dry steaks, hamburgers, pork patties, and chicken. This change need not increase the weight of the supplies and might actually reduce it a little.

RATION LIST: FREEZE-DRY UNITS ONLY ❹ ❺

A ration can be assembled by using complete meal units as put up by a few packers. It is the camper's Automat. A box or bag contains everything the packer considers necessary for four persons for one meal or day as the case may be. This is an easy way to feed a group but few people want to be fed in that way for very long. By this system weight is reduced to $1\frac{1}{2}$ to $1\frac{3}{4}$ pounds per person per day, time spent in cooking and cleaning up has been reduced to an irreducible minimum; but the cost per day has gone up substantially.

One word of warning—try out enough products of different companies to become familiar with them before placing a sizable order. As has been said before, freeze-dry products are not yet as standardized as canned foods in taste, appearance or size of portions.

It is hard to recommend such a ration for an extended time. It has built into it no real flexibility, no surprises and little variety. After a few days these meals would present great monotony. However, for short trips or single meals, particularly for the young or inexperienced camper, such a ration may have merit.

HIKERS' RATION LIST ❷ ❸

4 persons/two weeks; approximate weight 2 lbs./person/day

Bacon	24	lbs.
Dried beef	2	,,
Milk—powdered	4	,,
Fruit—dried	8	,,
Sugar	12	,,
Butter	4	,,
Salt	2	,,
Bisquick	12	,,
Pancake mix	12	,,
Cereal—quick cooking	6	,,
Cheese	4	,,
Tea	2	,,
Coffee—instant	2	,,
Lemon concentrate (1 plastic "lemon")	4	oz.
Dehydrated soup	4	,,
Dehydrated vegetables	6	,,
Rice	4	,,
Jam, honey, peanut butter	4	,,
Canned meats	4	,,

This is a very generous and yet not a heavy lot of food for young adult hikers. If it is supplemented with an occasional fish it is really an excellent hikers' ration.

NOTES ON RATION-LIST MAKING

1. Amount of food in camp ration lists should be figured larger in food value, not bulk, than for home use.
   Appetites usually are greater
   Emergencies must be prepared for
     Spilled pots
     Unexpected guests
     Abnormal cravings—these appear most unexpectedly
     Include substitutes for "fish not caught"
   Children's appetites change—may increase on long trips
2. Estimates of some items are hard to make and cannot be based solely on the number in the party. Example: A cake will not be changed in size because the party has three persons instead of four—do not reduce the baking powder in the list!
3. Make allowances for personal preferences of members of the group as far as reasonable.
4. Develop your own ration list for camping even in fixed camps—correcting it after each trip.
   Saves time in marketing
   Reduces routine work to a minimum both before and during trip
   Avoids overbuying and incomplete buying
   In a fixed camp—trailer or cabin—keep an inventory of foods on hand

An "emergency shelf" is valuable in all camping
When things are used from it replace as soon as
possible.

SUBSTITUTIONS

It may be of value to consider some of the most practical substitutions which may be made in the above lists.

Two and one-half pounds of *fresh meat* may be substituted for 1 pound of bacon. One pound of *ham* will take the place of about one-half pound of bacon.

Fresh eggs may be substituted for meat at the rate of 8 eggs to 1 pound of fresh meat or one-half pound of bacon.

One pound of *powdered eggs* is equivalent to about $3\frac{1}{2}$ dozen fresh eggs.

Three pints of *fresh milk* (3 lbs.) may be substituted for 1 pint (1 lb.) of evaporated. About 1/5 of a pound of *powdered milk* will equal one pint (1 lb.) of evaporated.

One pound of *fresh butter* is equal to one pound of canned. If butter is not carried, an equal weight of bacon should be added to the list.

Five pounds of *fresh fruit* are necessary as a substitute for 1 pound of dried. A one-pound tin of canned fruit will serve two or three men. One pound of dried fruit will serve approximately 4 or 5 men.

Fresh vegetables, with a few exceptions such as spinach, at the rate of 8 pounds of fresh to 1 pound of dehydrated, may be substituted for dehydrated ones.

Leafy vegetables, such as spinach and cabbage, require 16 pounds of fresh to make one pound of dry.

— 69 —

WEIGHTS AND MEASURES

Water—1 pint=1 lb.
Flour—4 cups=1 quart or 1 lb. (approximately, varies slightly with the kind of flour)
Butter—2 cups=1 lb.
Sugar—2 cups=1 lb.
Coffee—4 tbsp.=1 ounce
Beans—4 cups=1¾ lb.
Oatmeal—4 cups=⅔ lb.
Rice—4 cups=2 lbs.
Bacon—1 flitch (slab)=5–7 lbs.
Fresh eggs—1 doz.=1½ lbs.

MENUS AND MEAL PREPARATION

The kinds of meals will depend greatly upon the sort of camping one is doing and upon the individual tastes of the members of the party. As a rule, it will be found that a rather large breakfast, light lunch, and then the largest meal of the day in the evening are most satisfactory. This is a flexible plan. It is well suited to moving camps either on the road or trail. In fixed camps all members of the party are usually present for breakfast and supper but may not be at noon. A light lunch may be carried by the absent persons.

Whatever the plan, the food must be simple, nourishing, and such that it may be cooked quickly or in installments, if necessary.

Breakfast is an important meal from different points of view. The morale for the whole day depends in large measure upon it. Whether this meal is satisfying and "lasting" influences the success of the light lunch at noon. Nevertheless, breakfast may become stereotyped more easily, without losing its attractiveness, than either lunch or supper. Dried fruit, hot cereal, bacon, bread, butter, jam or marmalade, and coffee make a very good breakfast with a minimum amount of time being spent in its preparation. Prunes are, perhaps, most satisfactorily used for breakfast. If they are soaked overnight they require no longer to cook than does the rest of the meal. Hot cereals are to be preferred to cold and brown ones to white. Cornmeal mush may be used, but it requires long cooking. As soon as the fire is started, the fruit, which has been soaking, and water for the cereal and coffee should be put on. By the time the grub box is opened and the things necessary for the meal are assembled, the water will be hot and the cereal and coffee may be started. While they cook, the bacon can be sliced and fried and the "table" laid. If soaked prunes and quick cereal are used, the whole preparation of the meal should not take longer than twenty-five minutes.

Unless the members of the party are doing very heavy manual labor, they will be well pleased with a lunch at noon. Except when the weather is very warm, there should be something hot. Soup (powdered or condensed) or tea is often quite sufficient. Sandwiches made of cheese, cold meat, or jam, with previously cooked dried fruit such as peaches or apples, and chocolate, complete such a meal nicely. This sort of meal will require little time spent either in its preparation or in dishwashing.

The evening meal is the one which may be made a real event in the day's routine. It may be a complete dinner. Usually there should be meat, vegetables, dessert, and beverage, and perhaps soup.

Most likely the vegetables and possibly dried fruit for the

dessert will require soaking before they are cooked. They may be put to soak either at breakfast time or at some convenient time later in the day. Potatoes, corn, carrots, and apples require short periods of soaking. Those things that require long soaking and cooking may be started the night before if it is known that there will be little time to prepare the meal the next day. For example, beans may be soaked over night, and partially cooked while breakfast is being prepared, eaten, and the dishes washed, and cooked more during the lunch period. Consequently, they will need just a few minutes' cooking in the evening. If the party is in a fixed camp such things may also be cooked in a "hole" without requiring very frequent attention. ❶ ❷ ❸

Variety, however simple, is most welcome in the camp diet, and meals should be planned tentatively a few days in advance to insure it.

BASIC MENU PLAN

Along with the ration-list should go a basic menu plan. Here is the one which was designed to use the rations in Raup's Basic List:

Breakfast
    Stewed fruit (usually prunes)
    Hot cereal or pancakes
    Bacon
    Coffee, milk
Lunch—from this list but not necessarily all of it
    Soup
    Sandwiches
    Cheese
    Chocolate

Leftovers
Tea, milk
Dinner
Soup
Meat
    Bacon, ham, or cornbeef (fish, if caught)
Starchy food
    Beans, rice, potatoes
Vegetables
Dessert from the following
    Stewed fruit
    Pie
    Cake
    Pudding
Coffee, tea, or milk

An expanded menu using this general plan might look like this:

FIRST DAY

Breakfast	*Lunch*	*Supper*
Prunes	Soup (dehydrated)	Fried bacon
Rolled oats	Pilot bread	Potatoes au gratin
Fried bacon	Tea	Peach pudding
Bannock or bread	Chocolate	Bread—butter—jam
Butter		Coffee
Marmalade		
Coffee		

SECOND DAY

Stewed peaches	Cheese sandwiches	Corned beef hash
Cornmeal mush	Ham sandwiches	Harvard beets
Fried bacon	Stewed fruit	Dried apple pie
Bannock or bread	Cake	Cheese
Coffee	Tea	Bread, etc.
		Tea

THIRD DAY

Stewed prunes	Vegetable soup	Fried rice—bacon
Fried mush—	Pilot bread	Escalloped tomatoes
honey	Stewed fruit	Stewed fruit
Bacon	Chocolate	Bread, etc.
Biscuits, etc.	Milk	Coffee
Coffee		

FOURTH DAY

Stewed apricots	Corned beef sand-	Cream of celery soup
Wheatena	wiches	Stewed corn with
Bacon	Chocolate	bacon
Bread, etc.	Raisins	Green beans
Coffee	Tea, milk	Cottage pudding with
		chocolate sauce
		Bannock, etc.
		Coffee

FIFTH DAY

Prunes	Corned beef hash	Baked ham or fish
Fried fish	Bread, etc.	Mashed potatoes
Rolled oats	Tea	Creamed carrots
Bread, etc.	Cookies	Corn bread, etc.
Coffee		Apple dumplings
		Coffee

SIXTH DAY

Stewed peaches	Fish chowder	Fried ham
Rolled oats	Cornbread, etc.	Baked beans
Bacon	Raisins	Sour cabbage
Bread	Chocolate	Stewed fruit
Coffee	Tea	Cornbread, etc
		Cake & coffee

— 74 —

SEVENTH DAY

Stewed apples	Bean-cabbage salad	Fresh meat (if available) e.g. grouse pie or stewed duck —dumplings
Bacon	Bannock, etc.	
Pancakes and syrup (made in camp)	Tea	
Coffee	Chocolate	Rice
		Fruit—Cake—Tea

Chapter Four
GENERAL DISCUSSION
OF COOKERY

THIS CHAPTER is probably one which the reader will consider unnecessary when he first glances through the table of contents. However, here in one easily accessible place is a general discussion of common methods of cooking, particularly as they apply to camp cookery, that should prove useful to many neophyte campers.

WAYS OF COOKING

The principal ways of cooking food in camp are boiling, stewing, broiling, sautéing (commonly called frying), roasting, baking, and rarely deep-fat frying.

Boiling is cooking in boiling water. For most uses slowly boiling water does just as well as rapidly boiling water. Dehydrated foods, for example, return to their normal condition better and cook more thoroughly if they are cooked slowly.

Stewing is cooking in a small amount of water at a slightly lower temperature than boiling (*simmering*). Although this method requires more time than some of the others it is an excellent method for a great deal of camp cooking.

Broiling is cooking over direct heat without benefit of a pan. If cooking with wood in regions where hard wood is not available, lasting coals are out of the question and food is broiled over a small flame and what coals can be accumulated with it. The result is not so perfect but with care a very satisfactory product can result. If cooking with charcoal, the fire should be started probably 30 minutes before it is to be used. The food (usually meat or fish) is either placed upon a greased wire broiler or upon forked sticks in such a way that it may be turned frequently. It is turned when one side is seared and the cooking about half done.

This is, perhaps, the most favored way of cooking meat and fish in camp. The flavor is indeed superior but tender meat is required. There is also some loss of juices and fat—both of which are extremely valuable in camp cooking.

A simple method of broiling meats (but not fish) which permits saving fats and juices as well as being practical over a fire which has not or never will reach the stage of being a "bed of coals" is *pan-broiling*. A smoking hot frying pan is rubbed well with a piece of fat cut from the meat to be cooked. The meat is placed in the hot greased pan and turned as soon as it is seared on the lower side. Care should be taken in turning the meat that the seared surface is not broken and thereby the juices lost. A cake turner can be used or the piece may be flipped over with a fork placed under it.

Frying, in the true sense, is cooking in a large amount of fat raised to a temperature of 350° to 400° F. This method of cooking is not very well adapted to camp use since it requires the handling of a large amount of hot fat. However, for variety's sake, foods cooked by this method are occasionally quite welcome.

Lard and vegetable oils or fats are the most commonly used fats. The advantage of vegetable oils and fats is that the flavor of one food is not carried to the next. Great care should be taken to have the fat at the right temperature. If the fat is not hot enough the food will become grease-soaked and indigestible, or if it is too hot the food will become browned before it is thoroughly cooked. Only a small amount of food should be placed in the fat at one time; otherwise, the temperature will be lowered too much, and as a result the food will become soaked with grease. There is also danger of the fat boiling over the sides of the kettle if much food is added at once.

Rules for testing temperature of fat for deep fat frying: (1) When the fat begins to smoke, drop into it an inch cube of soft bread. If the bread becomes a golden brown in 40 seconds, the temperature is just right for frying any cooked mixture. (2) If the bread browns in 1 minute, the fat is the right temperature for uncooked foods.

Sautéing, commonly called frying, is cooking in a small amount of fat over a hot fire. Meat, fish, some vegetables, and some fruits may be cooked in this way. Meat needs very little fat if cooked by this method; some vegetables, such as potatoes, require more, and fish does best if the fat is one-half-inch deep in the frying pan. By this method food is cooked on one side and then turned and cooked on the other. Food so cooked is more difficult to digest than when cooked by most other methods. This is especially true if the grease is not kept very hot.

Roasting on a spit is cooking near a high heat—wood, charcoal, gas, or electricity. Meat or fowl is usually cooked this way—roasts of meat or whole fowl. The food is placed on a spit and turned slowly.

Roasting or baking in an oven. It is best to preheat the oven before placing the food to be cooked in it. If the oven has a temperature control no form of cooking is easier. Without such, it will take careful watching and practice before one develops the judgment necessary to produce a perfect roast. A small oven thermometer bought in most any hardware store is a good investment. Without a thermometer, use of the following test will help.

Tests for oven temperatures (if you have an oven): Sprinkle flour on a pan and place in oven to be tested. If it is *lightly browned* in five minutes the oven is *slow*. If it is a *medium golden brown* in five minutes the oven is *moderate*. If it is a *deep dark brown* in five minutes the oven is *hot*. If it is *deep dark brown* in three minutes the oven is *very hot*.

Modern practice calls for an uncovered pan for most meat roasting. However, a covered pan, even an improvised cover of aluminum foil, eliminates basting and "pot-watching." It is especially helpful in cooking poultry and pork.

Roasting in a reflector. Thin slices of bacon should be placed on top of the meat, fish, or fowl, and strips of bacon rind under it in a shallow reflector pan. A small amount of water may be poured into the pan to keep the fat and juices from burning. This liquid in the pan may be used for basting (pouring a liquid by spoonfuls over a roasting food to keep it from becoming too dry). The pan should be reversed occasionally so that the food may be evenly cooked. I have cooked a ten-pound rolled roast of beef by this method. ❷ ❸

— 79 —

Baking in a frying pan is perhaps the commonest method of baking used by present-day Indians of the north and others who are camping with little equipment. The main objection to the system is the amount of time and attention necessary to produce a nice bannock. Bannock is the food most commonly cooked in this way. ❷ ❸ ❹

In a greased frying pan place a small flat loaf of baking powder bread dough. Then hold the pan high above a hot fire, preferably coals, until the bannock has risen to about twice the original thickness. Lower the pan over the fire until the bottom of the loaf is lightly browned. Then remove the pan from the fire and prop it in front of the fire so that the top of the loaf can brown. If several loaves are to be baked, time may be saved by removing the first loaf from the pan when the under side is browned and propping it against a pan or even a board or log facing the fire to finish baking. The baking of the second loaf may thus be started while the first one is being finished.

Baking in a reflector. Place the reflector before a high hot fire. Watch carefully and when half of the contents of the pan is nicely browned reverse the pan and let the other half brown. Whether it is the front half or the back half which browns first will depend upon the reflector and the fire. Regulate the rate of baking by moving the reflector closer or farther from the fire as needed. ❷ ❸ ❹

Baking in a Dutch oven. Heat the oven and its cover, getting the cover very hot (not red hot, however) and the kettle quite hot. Grease the bottom and sides of the kettle, put in the bread, meat, or what have you. Place the oven on a layer of coals, put on the cover, and cover *it* with a layer of coals.

Replace the dead coals with live ones as needed. The amount of coals and time required for baking will have to be learned by the trial and error method. ❷ ❸

Baking in a hole. Dig a hole, roughly a little larger than the kettle which is to be used. Line the hole with stones if they are available. Place kindling in the hole and build a large quick fire of split wood. The object is to collect a large bed of coals and to heat the stones in the hole. Rake most of the coals out of the hole, place the covered kettle in the hole and place the coals over and around it. Cover the coals with 3 or 4 inches of earth. This method requires several hours or all night for baking. As in the use of the Dutch oven, practice is required before one is able to judge accurately the amount of coals and the length of time needed for a baking. ❷❸❹

HOW TO MEASURE

Accurate measurement is a determining factor in the success of a great deal of cooking. This does not mean, however, that all cooks must laboriously measure everything with a standard cup or spoon. Skill in judgment of measures comes with practice. Camp cooks are prone to scoff at measuring, but they usually have their pet cups and spoons, although they may be out sizes. The result is a cake with the same proportions as one made with standard size cups and spoons but it is likely to be outsized. Nevertheless, it will not be amiss to consider some of the standard measures and methods.

Measuring. A full measure is a level measure. When possible, flour should be sifted before measuring. In camp this is seldom possible, but care should be taken to keep from packing it tightly in the cup. Flour may be stirred with a spoon to lighten it. If the flour is packed the cup may contain as much as a fourth more than it should. Dry ingredients should be placed in the cup by spoonfuls until the cup is slightly rounded full, then it should be leveled off by scraping with a knife edge. A *tablespoonful* of dry ingredients is a *level* spoonful; of liquid—all the spoon will hold. To measure a tea- or tablespoonful of dry material, fill the spoon with the ingredient and then level it off with a knife. For a half-spoonful of dry food, divide the contents of the spoon lengthwise with the knife; divide halves crosswise for quarters; divide quarters crosswise for eighths. Divide a level spoonful crosswise twice for thirds. To measure a part of a spoonful of a liquid without special spoons, one must just depend upon one's own judgment.

Measuring Butter, Lard, etc. To measure solid fat, pack it tightly into the cup or spoon and level with a knife. If a fraction of a cup of solid fat is desired, a simple method of measuring is to fill the remaining portion of the cup with cold water, then add enough of the fat to bring the water to the top of the cup. For example, to measure $\frac{1}{4}$ cup of lard, fill the cup $\frac{3}{4}$ full of cold water, then add enough lard to bring the level of the water to the top of the cup. The amount of lard placed in the water will equal $\frac{1}{4}$ cup.

METHODS OF COMBINING INGREDIENTS

There are three ways of combining ingredients—stirring, beating, and folding. They are almost self explanatory.

Stirring is mixing by using a circular motion beginning near the center of the bowl and spiraling to the outer edge.

Beating is rapidly turning the mixture over and over with a spoon. This brings the lower portion of the ingredients to the top. It encloses a large amount of air in the food.

Folding is combining two ingredients by two motions— cutting with the edge of the spoon in a vertical downward motion and then turning the mixture over, bringing the back of the spoon against the bottom of the bowl each time. First the mixture is cut and then folded. These two motions are repeated alternately until the batter is completely mixed. This method is commonly used when combining beaten egg whites and a batter for cake. By this method air already in the mixture is prevented from escaping.

TABLE OF MEASURES

3 teaspoonfuls (liquid)	= 1 tablespoonful
4 tablespoonfuls „	= ¼ cup
1 cup	= ½ pint
4 cups	= 1 quart
1 pint (water)	= 1 lb.
4 cups flour (approx.)	= 1 quart or 1 lb.
2 cups butter	= 1 lb.
2 cups sugar	= 1 lb.
4 tablespoonfuls coffee	= 1 ounce
4 „ powdered milk and water	= 1 cup milk

More weight measures are to be found with ration lists, page 70.

TIME TABLES FOR COOKING

Boiling

	Hours	Minutes
Coffee		1– 3
Fish		
large (3–5 lbs.)		20–30
small (1–3 lbs.)		6–10
Ham (12 to 14 lbs.)	4– 5	
Cornmeal mush	1– 1¼	
Macaroni		10–12
Rice		20–25
Rolled oats (quick)		3–10
Rolled oats (slow)	1– 1¼	

Fresh Vegetables

Asparagus	12 to 15 minutes
Beans (string)	10 to 20 "
Beans (lima and shell)	20 to 30 "
Beets (young)	30 to 45 "
Cabbage	5 to 8 "
Cauliflower (whole head)	15 to 20 "
Corn (green)	3 to 5 "
Onions	10 to 30 "
Parsnips	7 to 15 "
Potatoes (sweet)	20 to 25 "
Potatoes (white)	20 to 30 "
Spinach	10 to 15 "

Broiling

A timetable for broiling is merely a guide, for the actual time varies in accordance with the heat of the fire and the distance of the food from it. Both these variants are difficult to standardize.

```
Steak—1 inch thick, per side .... rare—  5 to  8 minutes
                             medium—  8 to 10    „
                   well done—10 to 12    „
Chops  ...........................     15    „
   (Pork chops a little longer)
Chickens, ducks, other young birds ....     30    „
Wild duck .........................     20    „
Fish—slices ........................10 to 15    „
Fish—small thin .....................10 to 15    „
Ham—½" thick .....................10 to 12    „
```

Time Chart for Roasting

	Oven Temp.	Min./pound
Beef		
rare	300°	18–20
medium		22–25
well done		27–30
Pork		
fresh (*always* well done)	350°	30–35
cured, tenderized	300°	25–30
Lamb		
medium	300°	25–28
well done		30–35
Veal		
well done	300°	25–30
Chicken	300°	35–45
Duck (domestic)	325°	20–30
Grouse (prairie chicken)	350°	1–1¼ hr. (total)
Partridge	350°	½–1 hr. (total)
Pheasant	350°	15–20 min.
Rabbit	325°	1½–2 hrs. (total)

Duck— wild	325°	10–12 min.
Venison	325°	25 min.

Baking

		Hours	Minutes
Bread (white, small loaf)	.375°–400°	1	
Bread (graham loaf)	375°		40–50
Biscuits (baking powder)	450°		12–20
Cake (loaf)	350°		40–60
Cookies	425°		6–10
Cornbread	400°		30–40
Muffins	400°		20–25
Rolls (yeast)	400°		12–20
Bread pudding	350°	1	
Indian pudding	300°	2–3	
Rice pudding	350°	1	
Pies (fruit)	425°		30–50
Baked beans (in hole)		8–10	
Baked beans (stewed then baked in reflector)	mod.		45
Escalloped dishes (cooked mixtures)	mod.		15–20
Fish (thick, 3–4 lbs.)	400°		45–60
Fish (small)	400°		20–30

Without an oven thermometer a cook must learn to judge temperature in a different way. See page 79.

Deep Fat Frying

Croquettes	1–2
Fritters and doughnuts	3–5
Potatoes (raw, fresh)	7–8

TIMING ❶ ❷ ❸ ❹ ❺

How to have all parts of a meal ready at the same time. Inexperienced cooks complain more of trouble in having all parts of a meal ready to serve at the same time than in cooking the individual dishes. Perhaps the best way to alleviate this trouble is to plan the meal and order of operation well before the actual cooking is started. Then a time chart should be mapped out and any precooking preparations done. Then it is good practice to list either mentally or actually in written form, the things to be cooked in order from those taking the longest to those taking the least time. There will be an overlapping of cooking periods—at first only one item will be cooking but by serving time all items will be cooking and all will be done at approximately the same time. Suppose, for example, a meal is going to consist of a roast, boiled potatoes and spinach. The weight of the roast and the degree of doneness indicate that the roast must cook $2\frac{1}{2}$ hours, the potatoes will need 25–30 minutes and the spinach 10–15. So the oven must be preheated and ready to start cooking the roast $2\frac{1}{2}$–$2\frac{3}{4}$ hours before serving time. Then 30 minutes before serving time, the potatoes must be started but the spinach need not be started until 15 minutes before serving time. The starting times are all different but the finishing times are essentially the same. A little thought given to planning before the actual cooking starts is the secret.

Chapter Five
BREADS AND CEREALS

Breads

BREAD MAKING is one of the biggest and one of the most constant jobs connected with camp cookery. A camp without bread of any sort is a rather disappointing place; if the supply consists entirely of baking powder biscuits, baking is never done; and if yeast bread is used, the cook will spend about two days a week puttering with his sponge and loaves. Thus, if a bakery is not near, it seems that the only thing to do is to decide that bread is necessary and that it has to be produced in camp and then set about doing it. For a short trip it is scarcely necessary to consider yeast bread, and baking powder biscuits or loaves serve very well. For longer trips, yeast bread, although it is more trouble to make, is much to be preferred.

YEAST BREAD ❶ ❷ ❸

Liquid, dry, or compressed yeast may be used for raising bread in camp. The dry yeast foam cakes or packages of dry granular yeast are most satisfactory because they are more easily obtained and also keep much better.

LIQUID YEAST—WITH POTATOES

4 medium potatoes (pared) or equivalent of dehydrated	1 tsp. salt
	4 cups water
¼ cup sugar	1 cake dry yeast (or package of dry granules)
	1 tbsp. flour

Cook potatoes in the water until they are very soft, mash them; add a paste made of the sugar, salt and flour. Cook until the mixture thickens. Cool until lukewarm and add 1 yeast cake dissolved in a little water. Keep the mixture in a warm place until it ferments. One cupful of this potato mixture is equivalent to 1 yeast cake in making bread and one cupful may be used to start a new lot of liquid yeast.

BASIC YEAST BREAD

2 cups scalded milk (milk heated until bubbles form around the edge of the pan)
1 cup boiling water
1 tablespoon lard (or bacon fat)
1 tablespoon butter
4 teaspoonfuls salt
2 or 3 yeast cakes (or granulated dry yeast) dissolved in ¾ cup lukewarm water or the equivalent of liquid yeast
9 cups white flour or 1 white and enough whole wheat to stiffen
2 tablespoonsfuls sugar or
3 tablespoonfuls molasses (if whole wheat flour is used)

Directions for making yeast bread are very confusing to

most people unless they know already how to make bread and then they do not need directions. In the interest of clarity I am going to give the directions in outline form.

1. Soften the yeast in lukewarm water to which the sugar has been added. (Do not soften yeast in milk or water to which shortening has been added; this slows down the rising.)

2. Put scalded milk, boiling water, salt, and molasses (if whole wheat is used) in a large kettle. Cool until lukewarm.

3. Stir the yeast mixture into the scalded milk mixture being sure to keep the temperature at lukewarm. (If yeast becomes too hot it will be killed; if too cold, its leavening action will be very slow.)

4. To the mixture resulting from step 3, add about ½ of the flour. Beat until smooth.

5. Add, by beating, the melted but cool shortening.

6. Add just enough flour to make a soft dough which can be handled easily without having it stick to the hands or the board. Too much flour makes heavy tough bread.

7. Sprinkle the "bread board" with a handful of flour. (In camp a piece of oilcloth or canvas spread on a box or any flat surface does very well for a "board.")

8. Turn the dough out on the board and leave it alone for a few minutes. (It will then be easier to handle.)

9. Knead the dough until it is smooth and elastic—15 minutes. Place both hands on the dough, press gently down and forward with the heels of the hands. Make a quarter turn of the dough, lifting the edge of the dough with one hand and turning it slowly and slightly, while with the other hand fold the dough toward you. Then repeat this procedure.

10. Place the dough in a well-greased pan (twice the size of the dough).

11. Brush the top of the dough with melted fat.

12. Cover with a clean cloth and put the dough in a warm place to rise until doubled in bulk. *Do not* hurry this stage. When the dough has risen enough, a hole made by punching your finger in the dough will remain and not disappear immediately.

13. Divide the dough into portions for loaves (4 medium ones). Cover and leave on the board for a few minutes.

14. Shape loaves in long rolls to fit the pans.

15. Place in greased pan. Grease the tops of the loaves and if more than one loaf is in a pan, grease the sides of the loaves which touch each other.

16. Cover and keep in warm place to rise (until double in size again).

17. Bread may be brushed over with milk or butter before baking, to make the crust a darker brown.

18. Bake in a hot oven for 15 minutes then reduce heat and bake 35 minutes longer. Bread, when done, is well risen, nicely browned and if thumped on the bottom has a hollow sound. Two loaves which touched while baking should separate easily.

19. Remove loaves from the pans as soon as they are taken from the oven, and place side down to cool, preferably on a grid. If a crisp crust is desired, allow the bread to cool without covering; if a soft crust, cover with a cloth while cooling. The freshly baked loaves may be brushed with melted butter to give a delicious flavor to the crust.

OVENS FOR BAKING YEAST BREAD

In a camp not supplied with a stove, the reflector or Dutch oven offer the best means of baking yeast bread. If the Dutch oven is used, some time will most likely have to be spent in practice before an amateur is able to judge the temperature of the oven correctly.

METHODS OF KEEPING BREAD DOUGH WARM

In a camp where there is no stove or warm kitchen, the writer has found two methods of keeping dough warm. By one method, the pan of dough was placed in the top of a large bucket of lukewarm water. (The bucket was an empty five gallon gasoline can.) The bucket was then placed near a very small fire, or, on a very warm day, placed in bright sunshine.

By the other method a small Primus stove was used as the source of heat. Four stakes about 30 inches long were driven into the ground leaving enough space between them to hold the stove and the pans easily. (A space three feet long by eighteen inches is a good size.) A piece of canvas was then fastened around the stakes to protect the stove and the bread from the wind, and the top of the rack was partially covered. How completely covered depends on the weather conditions. The temperature where the bread was placed was kept between 85° and 90°. (A small thermometer is very convenient and can be placed along the side of the bread pans.) The stove was placed at one end of the enclosure and the pans of bread on sticks of wood at the other end. Bread made with an increased amount of yeast, as spoken of above, and kept warm by either of the methods just described can be made in camp in from six to eight hours even in cold rainy weather.

When the air temperature gets below 65° in camp, sour dough bread is more satisfactory to make since it will rise well even at temperatures near freezing.

SOUR DOUGH BREAD ❶ ❷ ❸

In a five pound lard pail, (or equivalent), mix 3 cups flour and 3 cups water. To this, add 1 tbsp. of sugar. The pail should be about only ⅔ full. Allow this to stand in a warm place until the mixture has fermented and become sour. Save about ½ cup of sour batter to start a new lot of sourings. To the remaining batter add about ½ tsp. soda (the exact amount depends upon sourness of batter), ½ tsp. salt, 1 tbsp. melted lard, and enough flour to make a very soft dough. Mix well. Put to rise. Let rise until twice its bulk and knead again. Make into loaves which about half fill the greased pans. Allow to rise until double in bulk, then bake.

To the ½ cup of sourings which was saved in the lard pail add flour and water until the original quantity of batter is mixed up. This will be sour and ready for use in a few hours.

This is the orthodox recipe for sour dough bread but if a yeast cake is added to the first batter before it is left to ferment the whole process is hurried.

SALT RISING BREAD (Very "Tempermental") ❶

2 tbsp. cornmeal	Flour
½ cup scalded milk or water	½ tbsp. sugar
1½ tsp. salt	3 tbsp. shortening

Mix cornmeal and milk and keep in a warm place until bubbles start to form (a day or two). Make a batter of 3 cups of flour, sugar, shortening, 1½ teaspoons salt, and water; stir into this the cornmeal mixture. Keep in a warm place until it has doubled in bulk. Work about 8 cups of flour into the mixture (adding a little more water or milk) to make a stiff dough. Knead until it is smooth and elastic—about 20 minutes. Shape into loaves and let rise again. Bake in a moderate oven.

OATMEAL BREAD

2 cups rolled oats	½ cup lukewarm water
2 cups boiling water	2 tbsp. melted shortening
¼ cup brown sugar	1 tsp. salt
1 yeast cake	Flour

Pour the boiling water over the rolled oats, cover, and let stand until lukewarm. Dissolve a yeast cake and brown sugar in lukewarm water, add the melted fat, and stir this mixture into the oatmeal and water. Add 1 cup of flour. Beat well, cover, and set in a warm place to rise until light (about 1 hour), when bubbles will appear.

Add enough flour (about 3 cups) and 1 tsp. salt to make a dough. Knead well. Place in a greased pan, cover, and let rise in a warm place, until double in bulk.

Make into loaves, and let rise until double in bulk (about 1 hour). Bake 45 minutes in a hot oven.

ANADAMA BREAD

1½ cups water	1½ tbsp. shortening
1 tsp. salt	1 pkg. granulated yeast
⅓ cup cornmeal (yellow preferred)	¼ cup *lukewarm* water
⅓ cup molasses	4–4½ cups flour

Bring water and salt to the boil, add cornmeal. Bring just to the boil again but do not boil. Stir constantly. Cool mixture, add molasses and shortening. Mix yeast in lukewarm water and add to cornmeal mixture. Add flour. Stir with a spoon until mixture becomes too stiff, then use hands. Knead and let rise (see directions under yeast bread, page 89). Punch down, place in greased pan and let rise until double. Bake in moderate oven 'till nicely browned, about 45 minutes.

ROLLS FROM BREAD DOUGH

To shape rolls from bread dough, pull or cut off as many small pieces of uniform size as there are to be rolls. Roll each piece of dough between floured hands until they are smooth and round. Brush with melted fat and place in pans. Allow to rise until double in bulk. Bake in a hot oven about 20 minutes.

CINNAMON ROLLS

Roll out a piece of dough until it is about 1 inch thick. Spread generously with butter (or bacon fat); sprinkle with brown sugar and cinnamon. Roll tightly like a jelly roll. Cut with a sharp knife into 1 inch pieces or slices. Grease the edges and place cut side down in a greased pan to rise. Bake in a hot oven for twenty minutes.

QUICK BREADS ❶ ❷ ❸ ❹

Quick breads are dependent on either baking powder, soda and cream of tartar, or soda and sour milk for their leavening power. Baking powder, of course, is more commonly used than either of the others because it is less bother than soda and cream of tartar and much more likely to be in a camp kitchen than is sour milk. With a good baking powder biscuit dough as a base, an almost endless list of variations in quick breads may be produced easily.

BAKING POWDER BISCUITS

3 cups flour
4 tsp. baking powder
1 tsp. salt
3 tbsp. shortening (bacon
fat does very well)

About 1–1⅓ cup liquid—all milk, equal parts milk and water, or all water

Mix dry ingredients, work in shortening with finger tips. If bacon fat is used, little salt will be necessary. Add liquid slowly, mixing with a fork or spoon to a soft dough. The amount of liquid necessarily varies, due to differences in flour. Toss dough on a floured board, or, in the absence of a bread board, a small amount on the bottom of a plate. Pat or roll the dough lightly until it is about ½ inch in thickness. Cut with a biscuit cutter, cup, or baking powder can top, or even cut in pieces with a knife. Place in a greased pan and bake in a hot oven, 12 to 15 minutes, or in a reflector in front of a hot fire for about 20 minutes. When those biscuits at the front edge are brown, turn the pan in the reflector. If baked too slowly, the biscuits will not rise well. This recipe makes about 15 or 18 biscuits, depending upon thickness and size, and fills an 18 inch reflector pan.

BISCUIT LOAF

Use preceding recipe for dough, using only water, sufficient to make a slightly stiffer dough than for biscuits. Make into two small loaves, handling as little as possible, place in a greased pan, and bake until a sliver of wood stuck in the center of a loaf has no dough adhering to it when it is removed. An 18-inch reflector pan will take a double recipe made into 3 or 4 loaves.

CORNMEAL AND WHITE FLOUR LOAF

Use the recipe for Biscuit Loaf, but substitute cornmeal for part of the white flour. From $\frac{1}{3}$ to $\frac{1}{2}$ cornmeal may be used according to taste. Make in same manner as when all white flour is used.

DROPPED BISCUITS

Use the same recipe as for Baking Powder Biscuits, except that enough water is used to make a dough soft enough to be dropped from a spoon on a pan without its spreading much. Bake as Baking Powder Biscuits.

BANNOCK ❷ ❸ ❹

The usual camp bread which is found in northern camps, that is, in the camps of men who are busy with something other than just camping for the fun of it, is most likely to be in the form of bannock. Bannock is really nothing more than baking powder biscuit dough of about the consistency of drop biscuits. It is spread in a greased pan instead of being dropped in the form of biscuits. The advantages of this form are that the large, thin loaf is more quickly prepared than either shaped or dropped biscuits and that it keeps longer without drying out. One disadvantage is that it takes a little longer to bake the large loaf than it does to bake biscuits.

An 18-inch reflector pan will hold biscuit dough made with 4 cups of flour, etc.

Dry ingredients may be mixed and then water or milk added to make a soft dough. The shortening is then melted and cooled *slightly* and added to the mixture last.

SODA BISCUITS

2 cups flour
½ tsp. soda

1 tsp. salt
2 tbsp. bacon fat
1 cup *sour* milk

Mix and bake as baking powder biscuits.

SODA—CREAM OF TARTAR BISCUITS

3 cups flour
2½ tsp. cream of tartar
1¼ tsp. soda

2 tbsp. bacon fat or other shortening
1 cup milk, or milk and water in equal parts, or water

Mix and bake as baking powder biscuits.

BEATEN BISCUITS

The old Southern standby of beaten biscuits would make a good camp bread if a person cared to spend the necessary time in making them. They approach pilot bread or ships biscuit of earlier campers.

5 cups flour	1 cup lard
1 cup milk or water	1 heaping tbsp. sugar
1 level tsp. salt	½ tsp. baking powder

Mix dry ingredients, work in the shortening, and add the liquid. Knead well and then beat with a bread paddle, rolling pin or flat side of an ax until the dough blisters. Cut small, thin biscuits and bake 1 to 1½ hours in a moderate oven. Beaten biscuits may be reheated. If milk is used the biscuits brown more nicely, but they also burn more quickly when reheated.

CORNBREAD

2 cups cornmeal	2 cups flour
3 tbsp. sugar	3 tbsp. melted shortening— bacon fat is excellent
3 tsp. baking powder	
1 tsp. salt	2 eggs—or equivalent in egg powder. If neither is available, they may be omitted without seriously injuring the cornbread.
2 cups or more of milk (enough to make a batter that will pour easily)	

Mix dry ingredients, add liquid and beat thoroughly. Add melted shortening; pour batter into a well-greased pan and bake 30 to 40 minutes in a moderate oven.

CORNMEAL MUFFINS

Cornmeal batter may be baked in muffin tins, if such are available.

CINNAMON ROLLS

3 cups flour
4 tsp. baking powder
½ tsp. salt
3 tbsp. raisins cut in small
 pieces

2 tbsp. sugar
4 tbsp. fat
About 1 cup water or milk
(enough to make a soft
dough)

Mix as for baking powder biscuits. Roll the dough about ½ inch thick and spread on it a little melted fat and a mixture of cinnamon, sugar, and raisins. Roll the dough into a cylinder (like a jelly roll) and cut off ½ inch slices. Spread the top of each with the sugar and cinnamon mixture and bake.

DOUGH-BOYS, FRY PAN ❷ ❸ ❹

2 cups flour
3 tsp. baking powder
½ teaspoon salt

2 tbsp. sugar
Water or milk to make a
 stiff dough

Mix dry ingredients and add enough liquid to make a stiff dough. Drop by spoonfuls into a frying pan which has very hot deep bacon fat in it. Cook until nicely browned on each side.

BAKING-POWDER BREAD MADE WITH BACON

⅔ cup flour
1 tsp. baking powder
Water to make a stiff dough

¼ tsp. salt
1 slice of fat bacon, finely
 chopped

Mix dry ingredients, add chopped bacon. Add enough water to make a stiff dough. Make into small thin loaves and bake in a frying pan. This bread may also be baked in ashes by completely covering the loaves with ashes and coals. The loaves may be wrapped in aluminum foil. Bake until a splinter stuck into the center of the loaf comes out dry. This is the bread that was originally referred to as "bannock."

PULLED FIRE BREAD

Work biscuit dough into long strips. Wrap these strips on peeled sticks (corkscrew fashion). Either hold the sticks over a hot fire and turn constantly until the bread is done, or sharpen the ends of the sticks and push them into the ground leaning so that the bread is over the fire. The sticks should be turned frequently.

UNLEAVENED BREAD

2 cups flour	1 tsp. sugar
½ tsp. salt	Water

Mix dry ingredients and add just enough water to hold them together. Knead thoroughly. Roll very thin, prick with a fork. Bake. This bread resembles hardtack and has the advantage of keeping very well.

PANCAKES

2 cups flour	3 tsp. baking powder
½ tsp. salt	About 1½–2 cups water or
2 tbsp. melted bacon fat	milk

Mix dry ingredients thoroughly and add liquid enough to make a batter which will pour from a spoon; beat well before frying. Fry in a hot frying pan or griddle that has been well greased but is not too greasy, which would make the cakes soggy. Three or four small cakes may be fried at once or one large enough to cover the bottom to within one-half inch of the rim. When a cake is full of bubbles and stiffened around the edge, turn and bake on the other side until that side is a light brown. Serve with syrup or honey.

SYRUP

1 cup water   1½ cups brown sugar
Boil until of the consistency of maple syrup.

EGG PANCAKES

2 cups flour   1½ cups milk or more to
1 tbsp. sugar   make batter that will pour
½ tsp. salt   well from a spoon
1 egg (or equivalent)   2 tsp. baking powder
                               4 tbsp. melted bacon fat

Add the milk to the dry ingredients and then add the egg (if a fresh one is used). Beat well and fry. Serve with syrup or honey.

CORNMEAL PANCAKES

1 cup cornmeal   Cold water or milk
2 tsp. baking powder   ½ cup flour
1 tsp. salt   2 tsp. sugar
                               1 egg

Mix dry ingredients, add egg well beaten, and enough water or milk to make a batter which will just pour from a spoon. Fry as pancakes.

SOUR DOUGH PANCAKES ❶ ❷ ❸

The night before the pancakes are to be made mix up a batter of flour and water (2½ cups of flour and about 2 cups of water for four people) and stir it into ½ cup sourings (see page 93 for recipe). The next morning add a little sugar, salt and soda (about 2 tablespoonfuls of sugar and ½ teaspoonful of soda to 4 or 5 cups of batter). The amount of soda depends upon the sourness of the batter. Beat well and fry.

DUMPLINGS ❷ ❸ ❹

Dumplings seem to give a festive air to the most commonplace camp meal. They also stretch a dwindling bread supply in a most effective way without calling attention to the shortage. They may be cooked with a stew, or cooked over stewed fruit.

DUMPLINGS I

Small baking powder biscuits either shaped or dropped may be cooked on top of stew or fruit. Fifteen minutes before the stew is done and when it is boiling rapidly, arrange biscuits on top of it, cover and cook rapidly for 15 minutes, taking care not to lift the cover, or the dumplings will be soggy.

DUMPLINGS II

1 cup flour
¼ tsp. salt
½ cup milk

1 tsp. baking powder
2 tbsp. bacon fat

Mix dry ingredients, cut in fat, wet with milk, making a smooth mass of dough. Roll or pat into a piece ¾ inch thick; cut like biscuits and arrange on top of stew. Cook as Dumplings I.

DUMPLINGS III

1 cup flour	6 tbsp. water or milk
1 tsp. baking powder	Salt
1 egg	Pepper

Mix dry ingredients; add egg; mix thoroughly and add liquid. Beat thoroughly and add to the top of a stew. Cook as Dumplings I.

Cereals

A hot cereal plays a much more important part in the camp breakfast than it does in the usual home breakfast. Quick cooking ones offer a good quick and easy breakfast.

PRECOOKED CEREALS (Quick Cooking Cereals)

The whole wheat cereals are to be preferred, usually, because of the more attractive flavor and also because of their slightly laxative qualities. Follow directions on the package. If the directions have been lost, try ½ cup cereal to 2 cups water. Bring the water to the boil after a pinch of salt has been added; stir in slowly the cereal and cook slowly for 5 minutes. If the resulting cereal is too thick or too thin correct the recipe the next morning.

CORNMEAL MUSH

2 cups cornmeal 8 cups water (for yellow
1 tbsp. salt meal, 4 cups for white)

Mix the cornmeal with enough cold water to make a batter
which will pour easily. When the remaining water to which
the salt has been added is boiling rapidly, pour into it the
batter, slowly stirring all the time. Stir constantly for 5 or
6 minutes; cover and move to a place where it will cook
slowly without burning for 1 hour. Stir occasionally. If the
mush becomes too thick, add *boiling* water.

FRIED MUSH ❶ ❷ ❸

Pour cornmeal mush, made by recipe above, into a wet mold
(pans or even coffee cans). Let cool and stiffen. Cut into thin
slices and fry in hot fat until nicely browned. Serve with
syrup or honey.

Chapter Six
SOUPS

THERE IS NO BETTER place to start camp cooking than with soups. Soups can be easy and quick or complicated and long in preparation. A soup may be a quick pick-up between meals or a really largish meal in itself. It may be simple or sophisticated. All this depends more upon the cook than upon a large variety of ingredients. The main ingredient is imagination. A cook equipped with just a few props in the form of seasonings can produce an ever changing array of interesting and good soups from a common camp larder.

Well chosen soups will fill a wide variety of camp needs. A simple mug of hot clear soup will give warmth and quick energy to a cold and tired camper. It may be the result of long and elaborate cooking of meat, fowl, bones, and seasonings or it may be simply a couple of bouillon cubes dissolved in a cup of hot water. A hearty soup of meat, fowl or seafood and vegetables prepared the day before a long or difficult day's trip away from camp, makes a good and ready meal for the campers when they return.

A common fault of most camp diets is that they do not include enough liquids. A cup of soup, however simple, at lunch or dinner, or both, will do much toward correcting this. If the weather is hot a cold soup can refresh a camper and at the same time replace lost liquid in his system. Some of the European fruit soups might be interesting to try.

UTENSILS FOR MAKING SOUPS

Kettle. One large enough to hold one-fourth more than the expected amount to be made. This kettle may be one of a variety of materials from heavy iron to an improvised aluminum foil cup.

Heat. Here again use may be made of what is available—small portion of a hot stove top; one burner of a gas, oil, or electric stove; small portable heater—sterno or gas; or an open wood fire on the ground.

BASIC INGREDIENTS FOR SOUPS

A selection of these should be in every camp kitchen.
 Bouillon cubes
 Soup bases, both beef and chicken
 Canned soups—unless weight is a determining factor
 Dehydrated soups
 Meats and vegetables—commonly found in the camp
  larder
 Left-overs—most important

SEASONINGS FOR SOUPS "A little goes a long way"

Salt	Onion—dehydrated
Pepper	Garlic salt or powder
Celery seed	Chili powder
	Curry powder

All of these are not put in every soup but rather chosen for a particular soup. A common much repeated soup may become a new one if the seasoning is changed.

SOUP ACCOMPANIMENTS OR GARNISHES

Variety of crackers. If source of supply is not difficult.

Chopped bacon bits. May be left from breakfast. Especially good with heartier soups such as bean, pea, and chowders.

Mint. chives, parsley. Either fresh or dried, good on many soups, either clear or creamed.

Chopped nuts. Cream soups.

Sliced sausages or frankfurts. Bean, pea, and vegetable soup.

Thin-sliced lemon or lime. Chicken soup and consommés.

Soured cream. Tomato and pea soups.

Left-over cooked eggs (even scrambled). Sliced, thin or shredded in consommés.

Grated cheese. Onion and potato soup.

Soups are generally divided into two groups: those made with stock; and those without it. Soup stock is the liquid in which fish or meat, fat, and bones have been cooked. Vegetable soups of one kind or another are the ones usually made with stock.

Many of those made without stock are called cream soups. Cream soups are made of vegetables or fish with milk and seasonings. They are usually thickened slightly.

SOUP STOCK MADE WITH FRESH MEAT OR FOWL AND BONES ❶ ❷ ❸

In camp any available fresh meat or fowl is used for stock. Naturally some kinds make tastier stock than others. There is a most desirable ratio between fat, bone, and lean meat which it is well to remember—⅓ fat and bone, ⅔ lean meat. Marrow bones, too, give a good flavor and much nourishment, so by no means discard them. Old birds including ducks, grouse, etc., are excellent for stock.

To secure some bits of juicy meat in the soup stock, cut about a fourth of the lean meat into small pieces, roll in flour and brown in hot fat (bacon fat does well). Add these browned bits and a few slices of onion, carrots and celery to the remaining meat in a large kettle, cover well with water and simmer for several hours—the longer the better—adding hot water when necessary.

Salt and pepper to taste should be added during the last half of the cooking period.

A scum will rise to the top of the water and it is frequently removed but this is a bad practice to follow in camp as by so doing a certain amount of nutriment is removed.

The stock will keep better if it is cooled quickly.

When domestic meat is used for stock in the home kitchen, most of the fat which rises to the top of the cooled stock is removed. In camp, however, this is seldom necessary for a person who is getting as much exercise as the usual camper can use quite a bit more fat than he would need under normal home conditions. It is also true that wild animals are seldom very fat and most likely it will be necessary to add fat to the stock rather than to take it away. A weak stock may be improved by reducing the quantity by boiling it down or by adding bouillon cubes or soup base.

SOUP STOCK MADE WITH CURED OR CANNED MEAT. ❶ ❷ ❸ ❹

The principle is the same as that for stock made from fresh meat. The amount of water used should be slightly greater. A ham bone with some bits of meat or corned beef do best.

Beef extract or bouillon cubes may be added for additional flavor. Stock from cured meats will take less salt than that made from fresh meat.

STOCK MADE WITH FISH ❶ ❷ ❸

6 cups water	1 stock of celery
1 carrot	Salt
1 onion	Pepper

3–4 fish skeletons, skin and heads. These need not be all of same kind of fish; whatever the fisherman catches.
Thyme, parsley, tarragon, and/or bay leaf (a *small*, *small* bit of these).

Simmer all for an hour or more. Reduce the quantity by boiling to one-third less. Strain and use instead of water in seafood soups and stews.

STOCK MADE WITH VEGETABLES

1 onion, thinly sliced	Salt, pepper
1 carrot „ „	1 cup canned tomatoes
2 potatoes „ „	3 tbsp. fat
1 small turnip „ „	Bit of thyme, parsley, tar-
1 stock celery „ „	ragon, or bay leaf

Cook onion in fat until it is tender but not brown. Add the other vegetables and water. Bring slowly to the boil and simmer for 1 hour or more.

Vegetable stock is best made from fresh vegetables, or

part fresh. If dehydrated vegetables are used, it is well to soak them for 20 minutes and throw away the water. Add fresh water and cook as fresh vegetables. Actually vegetable stock is only worthwhile if the camp cook has an over abundance of fresh vegetables. The water in which vegetables are cooked or that poured off canned vegetables should be saved and used in soups.

MEAT-VEGETABLE SOUP I (Fresh Vegetables)

6 cups soup stock
¼ cups diced carrots
¼ cup potatoes—diced
¼ cup celery—chopped
¼ cup cabbage—chopped
Salt

2 cups tomatoes—canned or fresh (skin removed)
1 onion—diced
Peas, beans, corn, etc., optional
Pepper

Add vegetables to prepared stock and cook slowly until they are tender. Long cooking improves the flavor. The selection of vegetables may vary according to what is available.

MEAT-VEGETABLE SOUP II (Dehydrated Vegetables)

Soup made from dehydrated mixed or julienne vegetables is very good. One cup of dehydrated vegetables to every 6 portions of soup is added to the previously prepared stock. Vegetables should be soaked 30–40 minutes if possible before they are added to the stock. The water in which they are soaked should be discarded. Allow to simmer for forty-five minutes or until the vegetables are done. Season as desired.

NOODLE SOUP

4 cups soup stock
1 handful noodles (broken into pieces)
Salt
Pepper

Add noodles to boiling soup stock and simmer until tender (noodles are tender when they can be cut with a fork pressed against the side of the kettle). Season to taste. Cooking time 30 minutes. *Variations*: Barley, rice, spaghetti, macaroni, or any thinly sliced fresh vegetable may be used instead of noodles.

CHICKEN CORN SOUP

1 quart chicken stock
2 cups diced chicken
1 cup corn—fresh (or ¼ cup dried)
Salt, pepper, pinch of powdered saffron (optional)
Combine all ingredients; season with salt, pepper, and saffron (*only* a pinch). Simmer 10 minutes and serve.

ONION SOUP

3 cups sliced fresh onions (or dehydrated onions measured after they have been soaked)
6 cups stock
¼ cup butter (bacon fat does very well)

3 tbsp. grated or finely chopped cheese (Parmesan cheese is best, but any may be used)
Salt, pepper
Toast or any dry cracker or bread

Fry the onions in butter until brown; add to the soup stock. Simmer for 45 minutes or 1 hour. If the camp stove has an oven the soup may be cooked in a covered pot in the oven. To serve pour the soup in bowls, place a piece of toast or cracker on top and sprinkle with the cheese.

CHEESE SOUP

4 cups soup stock
2 carrots (or ¼ cup dehy-
   drated)
4 tbsp. butter (or bacon
   drippings)
1 small onion (or few slices
   of dehydrated)
½ cup grated or chopped
   cheese
2 tbsp. flour
2 cups milk
Salt, pepper

Cook vegetables 2 or 3 minutes in one-half the butter, add stock and cook until vegetables are tender (about 20 minutes), add milk. Thicken with remaining butter and flour which have been rubbed together. Remove from fire and stir in cheese. Serve as soon as it is melted.

CHILI CON CARNE

½ lb. dry pinto or kidney
   beans (or 1 No. 2 can)
4 cups tomatoes
1 lb. ground or chopped
   meat (preferably beef—
canned corned beef does
   well, however)
1 large onion
Chili powder
Salt
Pepper

Cook beans (if dry beans are used) until they are almost done (about 2 hours); add meat, tomatoes, and onion and cook until meat and beans are done (about 1½ hours). About 45 minutes before the soup is done season liberally with salt, pepper, and chili powder. This soup is best if cooked long and slowly.

CREOLE SOUP

¼ cup rice
Few slices onion (soak
  dehydrated)
2 tbsp. bacon fat
2 cups tomatoes
¼ cup dehydrated corn

3 cups stock
1 tsp. sugar
Chili powder
Salt, pepper
Few slices green pepper
(either fresh or dehydrated)

Cook rice, corn, and onion, which has been browned in bacon fat, in the tomatoes and stock until done, about 45 minutes. Season when vegetables are about half done.

SPLIT PEA SOUP

1 ½ cups split peas
1 ham bone
1 carrot diced (3 tbsp. dehydrated carrot)
1 onion (or few slices dehydrated)

1 potato (or few slices dehydrated)
8 cups water
Pepper

Soak peas and other vegetables (if dehydrated) over night. Drain peas and vegetables. Combine ingredients and cook slowly for 2 hours. Stir frequently. If soup becomes too

— 114 —

thick dilute with hot water. No salt has been given in the recipe for the ham will probably be salty enough to season the soup.

DUTCH PEA SOUP

3 cups green split peas
3 quarts water
2 pigs feet (if available)
1 cup diced bacon (may be
  blanched)
3 leeks
2 onions

2 tbsp. butter
2 tbsp. chopped parsley
  (optional)
1 cup chopped celery with
  some leaves
4–6 frankfurters
Salt, pepper

Soak peas overnight in water. Then cook until tender. Add pigs feet and bacon and simmer for 2 hours. Wash and slice leeks and onions. Fry them in butter and add to soup along with celery and parsley and simmer 1 hour. Add sliced frankfurters last half hour. Season with salt and pepper. 'Tis best if it can stand overnight and be reheated for serving next day.

U. S. HOUSE OF REPRESENTATIVES BEAN SOUP

2 lbs. (4 cups) white soup
  beans
Pepper

Salt—if needed
Ham bone
1 small onion
Water

These small white beans go by a variety of names—soup, Michigan, Navy, etc. Cover beans with cold water and soak over night. Drain. Put in kettle with ham bone and onion, cover with cold water. Bring to boil and then simmer about 4 hours or until beans are very tender. Season with pepper and salt if needed. Before serving remove bits of meat from bone and mash beans with back of spoon.

SOUPS MADE FROM LEFT-OVER BEANS OR PEAS

Stewed or even baked beans can become a good soup if water or broth is added to dilute them and the seasoning corrected. The resulting soup should be simmered 15 to 20 minutes.

SOUP POT ❶ ❷

In a permanent camp there should be a soup pot into which all scraps of meat and vegetables find their way. This offers a never ending source of good soups—much better, frequently, than can be made upon a few minutes notice.

If the camp is in a warm climate, the "soup" should be reheated frequently and/or stored in a refrigerator. Great care must be taken that it does not sour.

With a little practice, a camp cook can produce superb soups although very little new or first run ingredients ever find their way into the pot. It is really a camp version of a "stock pot" as is found in every good restaurant, or the "pepper pot" of the tropics. Some families have been very proud of the age of the family "pepper pot" insisting that they have been going for as much as forty, fifty, or more years. It is thought that the things which made such age possible were the daily cooking and the hot spices used in the "brew."

CAMP COURT BOUILLON

This recipe is Southern in origin and good Southern cooks might cringe at what has happened to it. As it stands it has some things in common with Southern court bouillon and some in common with bouillabaisse. It is one of those recipes which can change with the supplies at hand and still be excellent. Here is a test of the use of the cook's imagination and flair for producing a new but good combination of basic ingredients. It may be soup or a stew depending upon proportion of liquid to solids.

1 quart fish stock—recipe page 110
¼ cup olive oil (or butter, bacon fat)
1 tsp. chopped parsley
¼ tsp. basil
¼ tsp. thyme
Pinch allspice (not enough to be recognized)
Pinch saffron (optional)
1 medium chopped onion
1 cup chopped celery
1 large chopped green pepper
1 bay leaf
1 large can tomatoes
½ lemon sliced
Dash of "hot sauce"
3–4 lbs. fish slices or fillets (any assortment of fish; ½ may be precooked shellfish)
1 cup dry white wine (optional)
Salt, pepper

Cook onions, celery, and green pepper in fat. Add them and the basil, thyme, allspice, saffron, bay leaf, parsley, lemon, and tomatoes and onions to the fish stock. Cook slowly 10 minutes. Add fish, simmer 15 minutes or until fish is done. Care should be taken to keep fish from breaking. Add wine last 5 or 10 minutes. Correct seasoning. Serve with French bread, toast, or crackers. If this "soup" is very thick it may be served as a stew over boiled rice.

Chowders

A chowder made with fish, clams, or most any seafood can be delicious and can be made the main dish for an excellent camp meal. This is one of the places where a fish stock can be used to good advantage—instead of part or all of the water called for in the recipe. Chowder is best when made a day before it is to be served.

FISH CHOWDER

2 slices bacon or salt pork (diced)
1½ cups sliced potatoes (if dehydrated, soaked)
2 cups fish, cut in small pieces

1 small onion, diced
3 cups water or fish stock
3 cups milk (diluted canned milk is best)
Salt, pepper

Fry bacon or pork in kettle. Add onion, potatoes, fish and water, or fish stock or mixture of the two. Cook slowly until potatoes are tender. Add milk, bring to the boil but do not boil. Serve with Pilot Bread if available.

Variations. 1) Canned celery soup may be used instead of part of the milk. 2) Stewed tomatoes may be used instead milk. 3) Seafood Chowder—canned clams, lobster, shrimp, including liquor in cans may be used instead of fish in any combination.

CLAM CHOWDER

3 slices of diced bacon (or ¼ lb. diced salt pork)
1 medium diced onion

3 cups milk (canned preferred); part of milk may be clam juice

3 cups diced potatoes
3 cups clams (fresh or
    canned—may be minced)

Salt and pepper
Butter

Cook bacon or pork until done; add onion and cook until onion is golden brown. Add potatoes and enough water to almost cover potatoes. Cook until potatoes are tender. Add clams. If fresh, cook 2 or 3 minutes; if cooked ones are used, just bring to boil. Add milk or milk and clam juice. Season with salt, pepper, and butter. Serve. *Variations:* Use basic recipe substituting cooked tomatoes for milk.

CORN CHOWDER

4 slices bacon diced (or
    diced salt pork)
1 medium onion finely diced
    (or soaked dehydrated)
2 cups diced potato

2 cups corn (fresh, canned,
    or soaked dehydrated)
2 cups canned milk—un-
    diluted
2 cups water
Salt and pepper

Cook bacon, add onion and cook 2 or 3 minutes more. Add water and potatoes and corn; cook until vegetables are tender, about 20 minutes. Add milk, simmer 10 minutes. Season and serve.

VEGETABLE CHOWDER I

Use recipe for corn chowder, substituting almost any assortment of vegetables for the corn.

VEGETABLE CHOWDER II

2 cups canned tomatoes
½ cup green peas
2 onions diced
3 cups diced potatoes
½ cup finely cut celery
1 cup finely cut carrots

1 green pepper finely diced
4 cups rich milk (undiluted canned is excellent)
3 cups water
Salt, pepper
2 tsp. butter

Cook onion and green pepper in butter for 2 or 3 minutes. Add other vegetables and water and cook until vegetables are tender, about 20 minutes (remember cooked vegetables need not be cooked and may be added with the milk). Add milk, season and serve.

CREAM SOUP: BASIC RECIPE

4 tbsp. butter
4 tbsp. flour
1 tsp. salt

4 cups cold milk, or 2 cups milk and 2 cups vegetable stock or chicken stock

Melt butter, add flour, cook 1 minute stirring constantly. Remove from heat, add milk or milk and stock. Cook until mixture thickens slightly. Season.

CREAM OF VEGETABLE SOUP

Add 1 cup of any cooked, mashed, or sieved vegetable to Basic recipe, above.

CREAM OF FISH SOUP

Add 1 cup flaked cooked fish to basic recipe.

OYSTER STEW

1 pint oysters including
  liquor
1 pint light cream or evaporated milk
2 tbsp. butter

2 tbsp. white wine or sherry
  (optional)
1 small onion
Salt, pepper

Look over oysters and remove bits of shell. Cook oysters in butter until edges curl. Add cream and bring to boil but do not boil. Season, add wine and serve. Fresh milk, dehydrated milk or half and half milk and cream may be used for a less rich stew.

POTATO SOUP

4 cups potatoes, finely diced
2 onions, finely diced
½ cup celery, finely diced
  (optional)
Salt, pepper

2 tbsp. butter
2 cups rich milk (or part
  milk and part chicken
  stock)

Cook vegetables in enough water to cover, until they are very well done. Mash vegetables in water, add milk or milk and stock. Bring just to boil, season and serve. *Variation—* Add 2 or 3 tbsp. tomato ketchup or chili sauce.

POTATO-ONION COLD SOUP

If the amount of onion is doubled in the basic Potato Soup recipe it makes a soup which is very good served cold on a hot day.

BREAKFAST SOUP ❷ ❸

There is really no good reason why soup would not make a good breakfast except custom. A breakfast of bacon and fried eggs may be difficult or almost impossible to produce over an open camp fire in the pouring rain. This soup is amazingly good and will satisfy the most fastidious. Try it!

2 cups soup stock (in an emergency 3 bouillon cubes in 2 cups of hot water)

1 egg
1 slice French bread (or 2 or 3 crackers)

Heat the stock or water to the boil. If water, add bouillon cubes. Cool slightly. Drop broken egg into liquid and poach (liquid should not boil). Place bread or crackers in bowl, lift egg from broth, place on bread or crackers; fill bowl with broth and serve.

COLD FRUIT SOUP

1 No. 2 can prunes (or ½ lb. cooked dried prunes)
1 No. 2 can apricots
1 No. 2 can cherries
3 tart apples

2 tbsp. cornstarch mixed with ¼ cup cold water
1 stick cinnamon
1 cup water

Cook fruits (almost any kind can be used), cinnamon and water until the fruit is very soft. Mash until fruit is smooth in texture (may be strained if sieve is available). Remove cinnamon stick. Add cornstarch (mixed with water). Bring to boil and boil for 2 minutes. Chill and serve.

VEGETABLE-FRUIT SOUP

1 potato, diced
1 onion, diced
1 celery stock, diced
1 tsp. curry powder
1 cup light cream or undiluted evaporated milk
Chives or peanuts

Salt, pepper
1 apple, diced
1 banana, diced
2 tbsp. butter
2 cups chicken stock (fat
 removed)

Cook onion and celery in butter for 1 or 2 minutes. Add other ingredients, except cream and chives or peanuts. Cook until vegetables and fruits are tender. Add cream and chives or peanuts. Season. May be served hot or cold.

BORSCH (Cold Beet)

1 bunch fresh beets (or 1
 No. 2 can)
2 qts. chicken broth
1 lemon—juice

Salt & sugar to taste. Try 1
 tsp. salt and 6 tbsp. sugar. Should have sweet-
 sour taste.

If fresh beets are used either beets or tops may be used. Grate or chop fine the cooked beets. Add beets to chicken broth; boil gently 8–10 minutes. Add lemon juice, salt, and sugar. Chill. Serve with sour cream, diced hard boiled eggs, chives or diced cucumber.

CANNED SOUPS

In the days when Horace Kephart's *Camp Cookery* was the campers' Bible, canned soup left much to be desired and stews took the place of soups in most camps. Today this is not true and canned soups have a very definite place in any kind of camp where their weight does not eliminate them. In such cases dehydrated soups, weighing only a fraction as much, are excellent replacements.

In selecting the brand of canned soup to be taken to camp, it is well to test several brands. Some brands have much better flavor than others, some are much more adaptable for uses other than "just open the can, add water and heat." It is better, also, to stick to a goodly supply of the simpler basic ones and rely upon changing them after the can is opened to suit the immediate need rather than try to take a can of each kind available.

The term "canned" may be confusing. There are "condensed" soups, usually in 10½ oz. cans and "ready to serve" soups in 16 oz. cans. For camp use "condensed" soups are preferable. Extra liquid can be added when the soup is used and need not be carried in the can. Condensed soups are excellent used as bases for quick sauces and gravies.

Canned soups can be the base for an infinite number of good quick soups. In some cases, canned soups of different kinds may be combined, the seasoning corrected, and an excellent "new" soup results. In other cases, odd bits of leftover foods may be added to a canned soup base for a new soup.

MINIMUM CANNED OR DEHYDRATED SOUP SHELF

Consommé
  Beef
  Chicken

Tomato (*not* Cream of)
Mushroom
Clam Chowder

Bouillon   Onion
  Beef
  Chicken

RECOMMENDED CANNED SOUP COMBINATIONS

Consommé or bouillon, *and* .... Almost any soup
Cream of tomato, *and* .... Vegetable
Cream of mushroom, *and* .... Cream of chicken
Cream of tomato, *and* .... Pea soup
Bouillon, *and* .... Tomato
Cream of mushroom, *and* .... Bouillon
Tomato, *and* .... Corn

DEHYDRATED SOUPS ❷ ❸ ❹ ❺

To prepare, follow the directions on the package to form the
basic soup. They are just as versatile as the canned variety
and can be used in the same way.

Chapter Seven
MEATS, FISH, AND EGGS

A DISCUSSION OF THE MEATS most suitable for camp use has already been given in Chapter Two. In this chapter it will suffice to give only recipes for cooking those meats.

A few general notes on the cooking of meat and fish may be helpful. Except in stews and soups, it is the object in meat cookery to keep the juices in. Consequently, the surfaces, except in those two methods of cooking, should be seared quickly. Likewise, except in the case of soups and stews, salt should not be added until the meat is almost cooked. In general, the most successful cooking of meat is accomplished without the addition of fat, and, in the case of roasting, with very little or no water.

Frying and broiling, either of which takes only a few minutes, are the quickest ways of cooking meat, while baking, roasting, and stewing or boiling are slower and generally take more than an hour. Only tender cuts should be used for frying and broiling, while tougher cuts may be used in stews.

In making soups and stews the temperature of the water when the meat is placed in it varies with the purpose for which it is intended. If meat is put in cold water and heated gradually, most of the juice is withdrawn, leaving the meat tasteless. This system is most often used in making stock for soups.

If the meat is put in boiling water and boiled rapidly for

a few minutes and then cooked at a lower temperature, the liquids at the surface of the meat are coagulated and the meat retains its juiciness. This method is best when the meat and not the stock is of first importance.

If the meat is started in cold water and quickly brought to the boil, then cooked slowly until it is done, some of the juices are retained in the meat and some are also found in the stock. This is the best method when both meat and stock are to be utilized.

Although in these notes on camp cooking most of the space has been given to a consideration of preserved foods, it seems advisable to devote a small amount of space to the cooking of fresh meats. A few sample recipes will be given and these can be used almost equally well with either "domestic" meat such as beef, lamb, or poultry or with game such as venison, bear, rabbit, or ducks and geese. Also, fresh meat may be substituted for cured in many of the recipes for cured or canned meats.

In general, either game or domestic meat may be broiled, fried, stewed, or roasted. If the meat is reasonably tender it is especially nice to broil, fry, or roast it. The tougher cuts are much improved by the long slow cooking of stewing and braising.

For recipes developed especially for game, the reader is referred to the files of magazines devoted to hunting and fishing or to *Camp Cookery* by Horace Kephart. (See bibliography.)

BROILED STEAKS, CHOPS OR BIRDS

Select only tender cuts of meat from young animals. Steaks or chops for broiling should be cut at least one inch thick.

Venison is usually improved by some pounding. Young birds or poultry may be broiled whole if they are slit down the back—cleaned, of course, before cooking!

BROILING IN STOVE

Preheat the broiler. Place meat on greased broiling rack. Place rack in the broiler so that the meat is 3 inches from the heat. When surface of meat nearest the heat is cooked, turn and continue cooking on the other side. Remove to serving dish, season with salt, pepper, butter and serve.

If there is a question of tenderness of the meat it is well to use a bit of tenderizer before cooking, using it according to directions on the package.

BROILING WITHOUT A STOVE

Broiling in a rack. Place the steak or chops or split-open bird in a well-greased wire broiling rack. Sear each side in hot flames then remove from the flame and finish cooking over a hot fire. When the meat is about half done turn the broiler so that the other side may cook. Season, when done, with salt, pepper, and butter if you have it.

Broiling on forked green sticks. Select a green-forked sapling of a wood which does not burn easily, such as most hardwoods. Sharpen the ends of the fork and run them through the meat in such a way that a large flat surface may be exposed to the fire. Proceed the same as when a wire broiler is used. ❸ ❹ ❺

Broiling on hot stones. Meat may even be broiled on large stones that have been wiped clean and then heated very hot. Avoid stones which burst when heated. When the stones are very hot pull them out to the edge of the fire, brush away the ashes, rub with a small piece of fat or bacon rind and "pan broil" on the stones or place the meat between two stones. When the meat is done season with salt, pepper, and butter if it is available. ❺

Pan-broiling. Meat may be broiled quite successfully in a frying pan. Heat the pan very hot. Rub it with a small piece of fat cut from the meat or with a small piece of bacon rind, so that the inside of the pan is covered with a film—a film and no more—of grease. Cook the meat until half done, turn and finish cooking. Season and serve.

FRYING (SAUTÉING) STEAKS OR CHOPS

Heat a little fat in a frying pan until it begins to smoke (use just enough fat to keep the meat from sticking to the pan). Cook over a hot fire until the meat is half done, then turn it and finish cooking. Season with salt and pepper when the meat is half done. Gravy may be made with the fryings in the pan. See page 130.

Steaks or chops may be rolled in flour before frying, in which case more grease will be necessary. Excellent gravy may be made after the meat is fried.

FRYING (SAUTÉING) CHICKEN OR GAME BIRDS

Cut the chicken into convenient pieces after it has been cleaned. (See page 135 for directions for cleaning and cutting.) If it is a young bird it may be fried without any previous cooking. A meat tenderizer can improve tough birds. If there is any doubt as to the tenderness of the bird it may be boiled until tender before frying. (The resulting liquid should be kept for gravy or soup stock.) Season the chicken with salt and pepper before rolling the pieces in flour. Then fry in hot melted fat. When the pieces are well browned (if they have not been boiled) it is often desirable (unless bird is very young) to add ½ cup of water to the bird in the frying can, cover and steam over a moderate heat until water is evaporated. This makes the tougher birds tender. In some cases it may be advisable to add water a second time. Some crispness is lost but even old birds treated this way are tender.

BRAISED MEAT

Cut meat into small pieces. Sprinkle them with salt and pepper and roll them in flour. Brown the meat in fat. Place it in a Dutch oven or a covered kettle, add water until it is about 2 inches deep in the kettle. Cook very slowly (simmer) for 2 or 3 hours or until the meat is tender, adding more water when necessary. Then add vegetables cut in pieces—potatoes, carrots, onions, etc. Continue cooking slowly until vegetables are done. The liquid in the kettle may be thickened and used as gravy. To thicken the gravy pour into the liquid a thin batter made of 4 tablespoons of flour mixed with a cup of water, or a thin batter made with 3 tablespoonfuls of cornstarch and ½ cup of water. The amount of thickening depends upon the amount of liquid in the kettle. Have the liquid in the kettle boiling when the thickening is being added. Use only enough thickening to make the gravy the desired thickness. Cook 3 minutes, stirring constantly. Correct seasoning and serve.

BRAISED CHICKEN, DUCK, ETC.

Clean and cut up the fowl (see page 135). Season with salt and pepper and roll in flour. Brown all surfaces by frying in bacon fat. Add 2 cups of water and a few slices of onion and carrot if desired. Cover and cook slowly until the fowl is done. The time depends on the age of the fowl. More water may be added as it is needed. Make a gravy by adding a little thickening to the stock in the pan. (See preceding recipe.)

FRESH MEAT STEW

Fresh meat	Onions
Potatoes	Salt, pepper
Carrots	

Amounts may vary according to taste. Mixed dehydrated vegetables may be used. Cut meat into medium sized pieces, roll in flour and brown by frying in bacon fat. Place meat in a kettle, add bone if one is available. Cover with water and cook slowly until meat is tender, about three hours. About one hour before the meat is done add salt, pepper, and vegetables. If fresh potatoes are used they need not be added until about 15 minutes after the other vegetables. A stew is extra good if dumplings are cooked on it (see page 103 for recipe). Chicken, duck, etc. may be used instead of meat.

MEAT PIE

Meat or fowl, etc.	Milk (if desired)
Potatoes, carrots, onion, etc.	Biscuit or pie dough

Cut meat or fowl into small pieces and boil until almost done. Place in a baking pan, greased reflector pan or Dutch oven with vegetables which have been partly cooked also by boiling. Add broth in which the meat was cooked and a little milk if desired. Season with salt and pepper. Cover with small biscuits (see page 96) or pieces of pie dough. Bake in hot oven until dough is done and nicely browned.

The vegetables and meat should not be boiled together for the vegetables will cook much more quickly. Leftover meats may be used instead of fresh. In that case stock or broth may be made by adding water to roasting pan drippings or stock may be made from soup base or bouillon cubes and water.

ROAST FRESH MEAT OR BIRDS

Excellent roast meat can be produced in camp by any one of several methods. Fowls or birds may be stuffed before roasting.

STOVE OVEN ROASTING: METHOD I

Place meat in an open, shallow pan with the fat side up and then put it in a preheated oven (see timetable for roasting page 85). Do not cover. Baste the meat occasionally with the drippings which accumulate in the bottom of the pan. Keep the oven temperature constant. Cook the time recommended in the timetable.

OVEN ROASTING: METHOD II

Some cooks prefer to sear (slightly brown) a roast at the beginning of the cooking period. It does give a good flavor to the meat, although the shrinkage in cooking may be a bit greater than if Method I is used.

The roast to be cooked is placed in a very hot oven (500°) and browned slightly. This takes about 20 minutes. Then the oven heat is reduced to 300° (or a slow oven) and roasting is continued. The shorter time given in the chart should be used for cooking a roast by this method. This time includes the searing time.

REFLECTOR ROASTING ❷ ❸ ❹

Season meat or fowl with salt and pepper. Sprinkle well with flour and place it in the reflector pan. Strips of salt pork or bacon may be laid across the top of the roast as may a few slices of onion, either fresh or soaked dehydrated. Place the reflector before a hot fire (one built with backlogs is best) and roast the meat until it is done. The reflector pan should be turned frequently so that the roast may cook evenly. A little water may be added to keep the roast from sticking. The liquid in the bottom of the pan should be spooned over the meat (basting) occasionally.

The length of time varies with the size of the roast and the distance the pan is from the fire. The times given for stove oven roasting are a good approximation but not exact.

Pared fresh vegetables, such as potatoes and carrots, may be placed around the roast and cooked at the same time. These should be rubbed with fat before placing them in the roasting pan.

Chickens, ducks, etc. are, of course, left whole when roasted. Wild duck is roasted a very short time—about thirty minutes. The flesh is red, not blue when done.

ROASTING ON A SPIT

Rotisseries—Electric, gas, charcoal. If meat is to be roasted on an electric or gas rotisserie follow the instructions which come with the appliance.

If charcoal or briquettes are used, a little skill and practice are necessary to produce good results. Judgment of the proper heat is gained by practice, although a few suggestions made be made: Do not have too hot a fire—meat or fowl should cook at about the same rate as if in a stove oven; Keep the heat constant.

On a spit before an open wood fire. A whole animal may be roasted when a spit is used and the fire built in a trench under it. However, much the same system may be used for much smaller pieces of meat, and quite successfully, too. Fasten the meat or fowl to a green stick which is supported above or near a fire on two forked sticks driven into the ground, one on either side of the fire. The stick to which the meat is fastened is revolved constantly or at least very frequently so that the meat is evenly cooked. The meat may be basted with a little bacon fat or butter or the following sauce, all of the ingredients being cooked together for five minutes.

2 cups vinegar (dilute with one half water if vinegar is very strong)	Salt, pepper
	2 tablespoons—butter or bacon fat
1 cup tomatoes	

Hanging from a tripod. A piece of meat or a fowl may be roasted by hanging it from a tripod in front of a hot high fire. If available, fasten a piece of wire (2 feet) to the roast and then use the string to fasten the wire to the tripod (the wire insures against the possibility of the string burning and the roast being lost). Seton, in *Arctic Prairies* (page 221) suggests: "A wire held the leg; on the top of the wire was a paddle or shingle of wood; above that beyond the heat was a cord. The wind gives the paddle a push: it winds the cord, which then unwinds itself. This goes on without fail and without effort, never still, and the roast is perfect." The drippings may be caught in a pan and used to baste the meat.

If there is no wind the cord would have to be wound by hand. Actually if there is wind enough to wind the cord, it is most likely that there is also wind enough to blow most of the heat away from the roast and to make the fire unmanageable and dangerous. So face up to it, and wind by hand!

STUFFING FOR FOWL

4 cups dry bread cut in small cubes	Sage (optional)
1 cup boiling water	4 tbsp. butter or bacon fat
Onion	Salt
	Pepper

Melt the butter in water and pour over the bread. Season to taste. *To stuff:* Put stuffing in the neck end until skin is fairly well filled (allow a little room for swelling of the bread). Fill the body cavity and bring skin together with a sliver of wood or sew with needle and thread.

TO CLEAN AND DRESS CHICKENS, DUCKS, ETC.
As soon as the bird is killed it is best to bleed it. It keeps better and also looks better. Turkeys, geese, and ducks are usually picked dry but it is simpler for the inexperienced person to scald them first like chickens. To scald a bird have a

large kettle of hot water (just below the boiling point) and quickly dip it in and out of the water several times. Care should be taken to make sure that all feathers are completely submerged. Then remove all the feathers by pulling them out by handfuls. Next hold the bird over a flame to burn off (singe) the hairs. Pinfeathers are removed by scrapping the bird gently with the back of a knife from the base of the feather away from the bird.

To draw a bird—cut off the head and the legs at the first joint. Make a slit from the base of the breast bone to and around the vent. Remove the entrails, gizzard, liver, and heart. The gall bladder is attached to the under side of the right lobe of the liver. Care must be taken to cut it out without breaking it or it will give a bitter flavor to the bird. (Pheasants have no gall bladder.) Care must be taken to remove all the lungs, enclosed by the ribs, and the kidneys, lying near the back bone. The windpipe and craw may be withdrawn through a small slit made in the skin at the side of the neck. Cut out the oil bag from the top of the tail. Wash the bird well in cold water.

TO CUT UP A FOWL

Cut through the skin between leg and body. Cut through the flesh toward the joint, bend back the leg and sever it from the body at the joint. Separate thigh, and lower leg (drum stick) in same manner. Likewise remove wings from body. Remove breast by cutting through skin on both sides of breast bone ridge up to the collar bone. Ribs may then be cut from the back. The wish bone is usually removed by cutting through the meat close to the upper end of the breast bone then downward and forward. Then break it loose. The back is frequently cut or broken into two pieces crosswise.

TO CLEAN GIBLETS

Remove membranes, arteries, and any clotted blood and veins from the heart. Cut gall bladder from the liver, being careful to remove any liver which has a greenish cast. Cut membranes from gizzard; cut through the thickest part to the membrane lining it. Remove inner sack and contents. Cut out openings from gizzard to intestines. Wash thoroughly.

TO DRESS BIRDS FOR BROILING

Split bird down the back and remove entrails, etc. Cut out ribs and remove breast bone. Clean giblets as above.

Cured Meats

Bacon

PARBOILING. Occasionally bacon is too salty and needs to be parboiled before cooking. This is done by placing slices of bacon in frying pan, covering with cold water, and bringing to the boil. Boil 2 or 3 minutes, pour off the water, and proceed with cooking.

FRIED. Cut bacon in thin slices (short slices fit the frying pan to a better advantage than do long ones). Heat the frying pan and fry bacon over a low flame or a few coals. (Coals, of course, are best.) As the fat fries out, it should be poured off. This makes the bacon less grease-soaked and prevents having burned fat for baking, etc. The bacon should be turned frequently and is done while it is still translucent. Do not be discouraged if your first bacon is over cooked. It takes a bit of practice to fry perfect bacon.

BROILED. Slice bacon thin and hold at side of coals until bacon is a light brown. The fat may be caught in a pan placed beneath the bacon. If no wire broiler has been included in the outfit, the bacon may be broiled on sticks. If electric or gas broiler is used, place bacon on rack near the heat.

BOILED. Place bacon (not sliced, but in one piece) in just enough water to cover. Bring to the boil slowly and simmer until done, 1 hour for the first pound and ½ hour for each additional pound. Remove the scum as it forms on the surface of the water. If the water gets too low, add more boiling water.

Boiled bacon, sliced cold, makes surprisingly good sandwiches. It may be toasted in front of an open fire or fried in the usual manner.

FRITTERS. Bacon fritters offer a good change. Make a thick batter of ⅓ cup cornmeal and ⅔ cup flour and a pinch of salt and ⅔ to 1 cup milk. Dip slices of bacon in batter, and fry in deep fat until they are a light brown.

Salt Pork

Salt pork may be used in the same ways as bacon. Generally it needs to be par-boiled. For parboiling see *Bacon*, above.

Ham

FRIED. Some ham is too salty and consequently needs parboiling. (See *Bacon*.) Then fry the same as bacon. Gravy made with the fat left after frying ham is delicious, especially if made with milk.

BROILED. Use ¾ inch slices, and broil them as bacon, about 10 minutes. Boiled ham is nice broiled.

BOILED. Wash and trim off all hard skin near the end of the bone. Put in cold water and bring to boil. Reduce heat and simmer until tender, 3 or 5 hours for 12 to 14 lb. ham. Time depends somewhat on type of cure. Let ham partially cool in liquor. Potatoes are good cooked in the liquor. The liquor may be used in place of ham bone for split pea soup unless it is a strong Southern country ham.

If the liquor is not wanted for making soup or cooking vegetables (and this is seldom the case in camp) a very fine flavor may be given the ham by adding a tablespoonful of whole cloves, a stick of cinnamon, 1 cup of brown sugar and ½ cup of vinegar to the water in which the ham is to be cooked. ½ teaspoonful ground cinnamon and ½ teaspoonful ground cloves may be used instead of the stick cinnamon and the whole cloves.

BAKED. Remove skin and some of the fat from a boiled ham. Place the ham in a baking pan. Sprinkle the ham with sugar (brown, if you have it) and bread crumbs, and stick cloves in it about ½ inch apart. Bake one hour with a rather slow fire.

BAKED WITH RUM. Place ham to be baked in baking pan. Sprinkle the ham with sugar and dry mustard (1 teaspoonful mustard to 1 cup sugar—brown preferred), pour a bit of dark rum over sugar from time to time until about ½ cup of rum has been used. Then baste ham with juices in the pan.

Dried Beef

SANDWICHES, sliced thin. Use well-buttered bread.

CREAMED. Break or cut thin slices of dried beef into small pieces—a cup full when cut. If the beef is too salty, simmer it for a few minutes in hot water. Melt 2 tablespoonfuls of butter or bacon fat in a frying pan; add meat and sear, stirring all the time. Sprinkle 2 tbsp. of flour over meat, stirring so that the flour is evenly distributed. When the flour is slightly browned, add 2 cups of milk and cook until the sauce is thickened. Little or no salt is required for there is usually enough in the beef.

Corned Beef

Corned beef is good sliced cold, or it may be cooked in hash or stews.

CORNED BEEF HASH. Chop cold corned beef with onions, either fresh or soaked dehydrated, and potatoes in the proportion of 1 part beef to 2 parts potatoes. Fry in bacon fat until a light brown.

Corned beef hash may also be baked. Place hash in greased pan in medium hot oven and bake until brown, about 30 minutes.

CORNED BEEF STEW. Boil potatoes and onion until they are about half done. Add one-fourth the amount of canned corned beef, broken into good-sized pieces. About 20 minutes before the stew is done place dumplings on top of it, replace the lid and boil rapidly. Make sure there is plenty of liquid to boil for 20 minutes. Season sparingly, for the corned beef is somewhat salty.

CURRIED CORNED BEEF. Break canned corned beef into pieces and reheat in curry sauce (see page 148). This is one of the most palatable ways to serve corned beef. Any curried meat that may be left from a meal is a fine addition to a soup pot. It gives a soup a new and delightful flavor.

Fresh Fish

To Clean Fish. First scale the fish, unless it is a trout which has no scales, by scraping it with a rather dull knife or the back of the blade of a sharp one. The strokes should begin at the tail and move forward to the head. After the scales have been removed, cut off the head, tail, and fins. Open the fish by making a slit along the ventral surface, remove the entrails, wash in cold water, and dry.

If the fish is to be broiled, it should be split open along the back and the back bone removed. Large fish for frying are nice if cut in steaks by slicing crosswise. Medium sized fish are often filleted. Small fish usually are fried whole, in which case it is best to sever the back bones to keep them from curling.

To fillet a Fish. Remove head, fins, and tail. Lay fish on a board and with a sharp knife cut through the skin and flesh along back to backbone. Then follow the ribs closely to ventral (or belly) side, separating the flesh from carcass. Turn the fish over and do likewise on the other side.

Fried. Fish may be fried in Crisco, bacon fat, salt pork, lard, or butter. The important thing to remember is to have the grease quite hot when the fish is put in, one piece at a time. Fish is usually rolled in flour or cornmeal. Either helps to brown them and prevents their sticking to the pan. Trout, however, are better if they are just wiped dry. Fish require much salt, the amount depending somewhat upon whether or not the grease has salt in it.

Broiled in Stove Broiler. Preheat the broiler about 10 minutes. Place the fish in a greased shallow pan. Brush top of fish with softened butter or bacon fat. Season with salt and pepper and sprinkle with a bit of lemon juice if it is available. (This helps to keep the fish firm.) The fish should be 2 or 3 inches from the source of heat. Broil until top is browned, basting a couple of times with more fat or drippings from pan. Fillets will usually broil in 5 to 6 minutes; steaks 1 inch thick will need 10–15 minutes. Do not over-cook.

Broiled in Wire Broiler Over Open Fire. To broil in a wire broiler, grease it and place the fish in it. A good bed of coals should be drawn out to one side of the fire and the broiler held over it. Do not cook the fish too fast or the inner portion will not be done. When the fish is nicely browned on one side—flesh side first—turn it so that the other side may be browned. When done, season with salt and pepper and butter. Melted bacon fat may be used to baste the fish while it is cooking, in which case butter need not be used.

Fish may be nicely broiled on sticks if no broiler is at hand. Green-forked branches strong enough to hold the small whole fish should be selected and the tip of the forks sharpened. The points of the forks are then forced through the fish lengthwise far enough to support the fish. The stick is then either propped or held so that the fish is over the fire.

Pieces of larger fish may be broiled on sticks but not quite so easily as the pieces are likely to break and be lost. If it is necessary to broil large fish, split the fish lengthwise and then crosswise into pieces of the desired size. This gives a larger piece of skin to help support the tender flesh.

Boiled. Fish to be "boiled" (really poached) should be rather large. The fish may be started either in cold, salted water and simmered, or it may be wrapped in a clean cloth and dropped into boiling salt water. Then reduce heat and simmer. As a scum rises to the top of the water, it should be skimmed off. Fish for "boiling" are not cut into pieces but rather left whole. The length of time for boiling depends upon the size and species; small ones usually take about 5 minutes per pound; larger ones require twice as long.

A few cloves, bay leaf, tablespoonful of vinegar or lemon juice, slice of onion or other spices or vegetables (celery, green pepper) may be added to the water for extra flavor.

Plain boiled fish is not very palatable, but may be made so by the use of a well-seasoned sauce or at least plenty of melted butter. See end of chapter for sauce recipes.

Oven-Baked. Place a cleaned and stuffed fish in the baking pan with three or four strips of bacon rind under it and lay a few strips of bacon on top of it. Rub with salt, pepper, and flour. Bake in a hot oven, basting frequently, until the flesh begins to separate into flakes. Large, coarse fish are best prepared in this manner.

Reflector-Baked. Prepare as above. Place in reflector and bake before a hot fire.

Stuffing. Brown 1½ cupfuls of bread cubes in 4 tablespoons of butter or bacon fat; then add enough water to moisten them slightly. Season well with salt, pepper, a small amount of onion and a bit of poultry dressing. Stuff the fish and sew up the opening or tie it well with string.

Planked. Split out a slab of hard wood 2 inches thick and a little longer and wider than the fish to be cooked. Prop the slab in front of a hot fire until it is very hot, then grease it. When cleaning the fish, split it down the back instead of down the belly side. Spread the fish out on the plank, skin side down, and fasten it to the plank with nails. Then prop it before the fire. Baste frequently with butter or bacon fat. Change the position of the plank, when it is necessary, in order to secure even cooking. When the flesh is flaky, the fish is done. Season with salt, pepper, and butter or bacon fat.

Canned or Cured Fish

CODFISH IN WHITE SAUCE

Melt 2 tablespoons of butter in frying pan and add 1 tablespoon flour, stirring constantly until well cooked; add 2 cups
of milk, and pepper; cook for 3 or 4 minutes. Add 1 cup of
salt codfish flakes, which have been freshened. To freshen
cover the fish flakes with cold water and heat quickly to the
boiling point. Repeat this until the fish is not salty. Drain
and add fish to the sauce. Reheat and serve on toast, rice, or
baked potato.

CODFISH BALLS

If the canned, prepared balls are used, follow directions on
the can. If the balls are to be made from salt codfish, soak it
for several hours in cold water. Cook the fish, mix with
mashed potatoes in the proportion of 1 cup fish to 2 cups of
potatoes. Mix the fish and potatoes thoroughly, season with
pepper, make into balls and fry, preferably in deep fat.

CODFISH HASH

1 cup flaked salt cod	Bacon fat
2 cups diced raw potatoes	Pepper

Freshen cod (as in recipe for creamed cod), add to potatoes
and boil until the potatoes are soft. Drain, mash, and brown
in bacon fat in a frying pan.

CANNED SALMON—COLD

Canned salmon is very good cold, just as it comes from the
can. If vinegar or lemon are available, they make pleasing
condiments for it.

CREAMED SALMON

Flake the salmon and add half as much milk as there is salmon. Bring to a boil and season with salt, pepper, and butter. Any cold cooked fish may be used instead of salmon.

SALMON CROQUETTES

Drain and save the liquid from a can of salmon. Shred or mash the salmon with a fork, then mix it with bread or cracker crumbs, 1 egg (or equivalent in dehydrated), and a little milk until of a consistency which will hold together when made into cakes. Season with onion, salt, and pepper. Shape into croquettes. Fry in Crisco or bacon fat.

SALMON LOAF

Instead of making the mixture in the preceding recipe into croquettes, make into a loaf and bake.

SALMON SAUCE

Make a white sauce (see page 147), using the liquid which was on the salmon in place of part of the milk.

SALMON IN SOUR CREAM

1 No. 2 can red salmon	Lemon juice
1 cup naturally soured cream	Paprika

Pour salmon into a shallow baking dish. Remove bones. Sprinkle with lemon juice. Pour sour cream on top. Bake in a slow oven (300–325°) until cream reduces and gets splotched with brown. Serve over boiled rice.

SARDINES

Sardines make a good pickup lunch used in sandwiches, and most everyone likes them. There are also a number of other ways of using them which are worth considering.

FRIED SARDINES

Drain and wipe the oil from the sardines, thoroughly heat in a frying pan (a very small amount of butter or bacon fat may be needed) and serve with hot biscuits or toasted pilot bread.

CREAMED SARDINES

Drain and wipe the oil from the sardines, then follow the directions for creamed salmon.

THICKENED GRAVY

After meat has been fried, pour out all of the grease except 2 tablespoons into which rub 1 tablespoon of flour. Stir and rub constantly until well browned (if white gravy is desired, do not brown); remove from fire and add 2 cups of cold water or milk or ½ water and ½ milk. Season with salt and pepper and let it boil up well.

BUTTER SAUCE

1 tbsp. butter   1 cup boiling water
1½ tbsp. flour   Salt, pepper

Put butter in a cold pan and rub the flour into it. Add boiling water, seasoning, and boil 2 minutes. This sauce should be used while hot. Good with fish.

MUSTARD SAUCE

Melt 3 tablespoons butter; stir in 1 tablespoon flour and
½ teaspoon dry mustard. Add 1 cup broth or water, salt
and pepper. Bring to a boil and serve. This is very good with
boiled fish or canned meats.

WHITE SAUCE—THIN

1 tbsp. fat	1 cup hot milk (scald if
1 tbsp. flour	fresh milk is used)
	¼ tsp. salt
	Pepper

To the melted fat in a frying pan add the flour and stir well.
Remove from the fire, add the milk, slowly, stirring constantly. Season and bring to the boil. If cold milk is used it
maybe added more rapidly. It is sometimes easier to make
a smooth sauce by this method. Milk made from powdered
milk does not need to be scalded. *To scald milk:* Heat milk
until bubbles appear around the edge of the pan.

WHITE SAUCE—MEDIUM

2 tbsp. fat	2 tbsp. flour
1 cup milk	Salt, pepper

Prepare in same manner as THIN WHITE SAUCE, above.

WHITE SAUCE—THICK

Prepare in same manner as THIN WHITE SAUCE, above, but
use 3 tbsp. fat and 3 tbsp. flour.

SIMPLE CURRY SAUCE NO. 1

1 small onion (or equiv-
    alent in dehydrated)
2 tbsp. butter or bacon fat
1 tbsp. flour

1 tbsp. curry powder (or
    more according to taste)
2 cups broth or water

Brown onion in bacon fat, add flour and cook. Pour the broth in slowly, stirring constantly, so it doesn't become lumpy. Cook slowly for 15 minutes; add the meat or vegetables to be curried and let stand in a warm place 20–30 minutes to thoroughly season.

CURRY SAUCE NO. 2

1 cup chopped fresh onion
    (or soaked dehydrated)
¼ cup chopped carrot
    (or soaked dehydrated)
¼ cup chopped celery
    (or soaked dehydrated)
1 chopped apple
    (or soaked dehydrated)

2 tbsp. tomato paste
3 cups chicken broth
3 tsp. flour
1 tsp. curry powder or more
3 tsp. fat, Crisco or bacon
Salt, pepper

Melt fat, add vegetables and apple, cook for 3 to 5 minutes. Sprinkle with curry powder, cook 2–3 minutes, stirring constantly. Add flour, sprinkling it over the vegetables and apple. Add broth into which the tomato paste has been stirred. Bring to boil, then simmer 30 minutes. Correct the seasoning. Sauce may be strained to remove vegetables and fruit.

Eggs

DEHYDRATED EGGS

Dehydrated eggs should be soaked in cold water as directed on the package. These eggs may be used as fresh eggs in baking and with fair success as scrambled eggs or in omelets.

BOILED EGGS (CODDLED)

Place the eggs in a pan of boiling water (sufficient water to cover the eggs well). Cover and remove the pan to the edge of the fire where it will keep hot but not boil. Cook thus for 6 to 8 minutes for "soft boiled" eggs or 20 to 25 minutes for "hard boiled" eggs. If eggs are really boiled the white becomes quite tough and they are less easily digested.

POACHED EGGS

Fill a frying pan two-thirds full with salted water (1 teaspoonful salt to one pint of water). Bring the water to the boil. Break each egg to be cooked in a cup separately and carefully slip each into the pan of water. There should be enough water to cover the eggs. The temperature of the water should be kept just below the boiling point. When the white is firm they are done. Care must be taken in removing them (with a large spoon or pancake turner) or they may be broken. Poached eggs are especially good with corned beef hash and spinach.

FRIED EGGS

Heat a frying pan. Put in it a small amount of butter, bacon fat, or other fat; when melted, drop in an egg which has been carefully broken in a cup, and cook over a moderate fire until the white is firm. If desired the egg may be turned once. Add more fat as needed to keep the eggs from sticking. The pan may be covered while eggs are cooking. These are a cross between fried and poached.

Eggs fried after ham is cooked (in same pan) are very good, but it is sometimes difficult to keep them from sticking.

SCRAMBLED EGGS

5 eggs   ¼ cup milk—or preferably
½ tsp. salt   cream
2 tbsp. butter or bacon fat   Pepper

Beat eggs slightly with a fork; add salt, pepper, and milk. Melt butter in the frying pan and add egg mixture. Cook over a low fire until the mixture is of a creamy consistency, stirring constantly and scraping well from the bottom and sides of the pan. Chopped cooked bacon, ham, dried beef, potatoes, tomatoes, etc. may be added to scrambled eggs.

FRENCH OMELET

3 eggs   ½ tsp. salt
3 tbsp. water   Pepper
2 tbsp. butter

Use a heavy pan. Beat eggs slightly, just enough to blend yolks and whites. Add water and seasoning. Melt butter in hot pan. Add egg mixture. Reduce heat a bit. As the omelet cooks, tip the pan and lift edges of omelet so the uncooked part may run under the cooked. When egg mixture is set, fold one half over the other and serve.

PUFFY OMELET

4 eggs	4 tbsp. water
½ tsp. salt	1 tbsp. butter or bacon fat
Pepper	

Separate yolks and whites of the eggs. Add salt, pepper, and water to the yolks and beat well. Cut and fold in the whites which have been beaten until stiff. Heat a little butter or fat in a frying pan, making sure that the sides are well greased. Pour in the egg mixture and cook slowly over a *low* fire until the omelet is well puffed up and slightly browned underneath. If one has an oven, place pan and omelet in moderate oven until upper surface is dry to touch. Without an oven hold the pan slightly tilted in front of a high fire until the upper surface is dry to the touch. With a knife make 2 short incisions in the omelet at opposite sides and carefully fold one half over the other. Serve at once.

Omelets are tricky but really good ones *can* be made over an open fire in camp.

Fillings. Omelets may be served with white or cheese sauce. Bits of cooked meats or vegetables may be added to the sauce. Cooked or uncooked fruits or vegetables, cooked, chopped meats, or jelly or jam, etc., may be folded in an omelet.

BAKED EGGS

Grease baking pan and slip into it the desired number of eggs. Add a little milk, about 1 tablespoonful for each egg. Sprinkle the eggs with grated cheese, salt and pepper. Bake in low heat until eggs are firm. This recipe is only practical when the size of the baking pan is well suited to the number of eggs desired.

EGGS ROASTED IN ASHES

Crack the shells of the eggs a little at one end (otherwise they will explode) and place them in hot ashes or embers so they are completely covered. Cook a very few minutes.

Chapter Eight
VEGETABLES AND SALADS

Fresh Vegetables. Fresh vegetables should be washed thoroughly and are usually peeled, or young ones scraped before they are cooked. However, if the vegetables are to be boiled, it is just as well not to peel them until after they are cooked. This method is more economical of both nutritive material and quantity of vegetable lost in preparation.

Canned Vegetables. Contrary to the belief prevalent a few years ago, the liquid on canned vegetables is of great food value. If it is impractical to serve all of the liquid with the vegetables, it may be kept and used in soups and sauces.

Dehydrated Vegetables. When it is possible, dehydrated vegetables should be soaked in cold or lukewarm water before cooking. They are then more tender and more quickly cooked. If they are cooked without previous soaking, they should be cooked slowly, and will require a little more water. If the dehydrated flavor is very noticeable, they should be cooked in fresh water and not that in which they soaked.

Methods of cleaning vegetables that are sandy or have insects on them. Soak for 30 minutes or longer in salt water, 1 tablespoon of salt to 2 qts. (8 cups) of water. Then wash carefully through many waters.

FRESH BOILED POTATOES

Select fresh potatoes of approximately the same size or cut them so the pieces are of uniform size. Remove the eyes and any discolored spots and, if it is impractical to cook them without paring them, pare them as thinly as possible. The water in which they are to be cooked should be boiling rapidly. After the potatoes are added, the heat may be regulated so that the water still boils steadily but slowly. When almost done, salt may be added to the water. The length of time required to boil potatoes depends upon the age and variety used. Old ones usually cook in about 30 or 40 minutes, while new ones cook in 20 to 25 minutes. If the potatoes are large, the outside often is done while the center is still hard. To finish cooking such potatoes, add 2 cups of cold water. When done, drain them and keep uncovered in a warm place until they are to be eaten. The water in which pared potatoes are boiled may be used for sponge in bread making (see page 89).

FRESH STEAMED POTATOES

Prepare as for boiling, but cook over boiling water for 40 minutes in such a way that the steam can pass around them. This method is not very practical for most camp cooking.

MASHED POTATOES

Boil potatoes until well cooked; drain from water. After draining, the potatoes should be placed over the heat for a few minutes to dry them. Then mash them until no lumps remain. In camp a potato masher may be improvised by peeling the bark from a green stick about 3 inches in diameter and 10 inches long, and whittling it into the shape of bottle with a long neck. A wide-bottomed, narrow-necked bottle also does very well, if care is taken not to break it.

To five medium-sized potatoes, add 1 teaspoon of salt, a pinch of baking powder, a bit of pepper, and ⅓ cup of hot milk; beat until light. Butter may be added if desired and available.

FRESH BAKED POTATOES

Nessmuk's recipe: "Scoop out a basin-like depression under the fore-stick, 3 or 4 inches deep, and large enough to hold the tubers when laid side by side; fill it with bright hardwood coals and keep up a strong heat for ½ hour or more. Next, clean out the hole and put the potatoes in it, and cover them with hot sand or ashes, topped with a heap of glowing coals, and keep up all the heat you can. In about 40 minutes commence to try them with a sharpened hardwood sliver; when this will pass through them, they are done and should be raked out at once. Run the sliver through them from end to end, to let the steam escape and use immediately, as a roast potato quickly becomes soggy and bitter." (*Woodcraft* by Nessmuk, p. 12).

FRESH RAW POTATOES, FRIED

Peel and slice potatoes into thin slices. Fry in bacon fat and season with salt and pepper. Raw potatoes require more fat than cooked ones.

COOKED POTATOES, FRIED

Slice boiled, steamed, or baked potatoes (with skins on) that have been left over into thin slices, and fry in bacon fat.

DEHYDRATED POTATOES, FRIED

Soak dehydrated potatoes for about 1 hour, then dry with a cloth and fry as if they were fresh. Usually, however, boiling dehydrated potatoes until they are almost done before frying makes better fried potatoes.

FRENCH FRIED POTATOES

Wash and pare potatoes, cut into $\frac{1}{4}$ inch sticks (or smaller if desired) and soak one hour in cold water. (Soaked dehydrated potatoes may be used.) Drain and dry thoroughly and fry a few at a time in deep fat until well browned. Drain and season with salt. This method is not very practical for most camps.

POTATOES FRIED WITH ONIONS

Pare and slice 2 or 3 medium-sized onions for every 6 medium-sized potatoes and fry them as in the precedings three recipes.

ESCALLOPED POTATOES

Wash, pare, and cut potatoes in $\frac{1}{4}$ inch slices (soaked dehydrated potatoes may be used). Put a layer of potatoes into a greased baking pan, season with salt and pepper and sprinkle a little flour over them; repeat until the required amount of potatoes has been used. Add hot milk until it shows clearly through the top layer of potatoes. Bake until potatoes are done, about 1½ hours.

ESCALLOPED POTATOES WITH CHEESE

Proceed the same as in the preceding recipe and sprinkle each layer of potatoes generously with cheese either grated or cut very fine.

ESCALLOPED POTATOES WITH HAM OR FRESH CHOPS

Place a layer of chopped ham over every two layers of potatoes in recipe above, or place a slice of ham or fresh chops over the top layer of potatoes. (Omit cheese.)

POTATOES ROASTED WITH MEAT

Place medium sized pared fresh potatoes around a roast of meat in the bake pan when the meat is placed in oven. Baste every 15 minutes with drippings from the meat.

POTATO CAKES

Cold mashed potatoes may be made into small flat cakes, rolled in flour or dipped in well-beaten egg, and then in fine cracker or bread crumbs and browned in hot fat.

CREAMED POTATOES NO. 1

Reheat cold boiled or baked potatoes, cut in cubes, in medium white sauce. Season with salt and pepper. Let stand in warm place for 30 minutes.

CREAMED POTATOES NO. 2

Reheat cooked potato cubes in enough cream to cover. Season with salt and pepper. If the camp has a double boiler, the potatoes in cream may be cooked slowly until most of cream is absorbed. Baked potatoes are excellent if cooked this way.

POTATOES AU GRATIN

Put creamed potatoes in buttered bake pan, cover with crumbs, and bake until crumbs are browned. Grated cheese may be added to the creamed potatoes.

HASHED BROWN POTATOES

Melt 3 tablespoonfuls of bacon fat in frying pan. Add 2 cups of chopped boiled potatoes, a little salt and pepper; cook about 3 minutes, stirring constantly. Let stand to brown underneath. Fold as an omelet and serve.

SWEET POTATOES

Boiled. Wash potatoes of uniform size and boil them until they are almost done (just a little hard in the center). Then pour water off, cover kettle, and let stand (may hang at edge of camp fire) in a warm place where they may steam for 10 minutes. Sometimes the potatoes are pared and cooked in as little water as possible. When they are done, brown sugar and butter are added, after which they are cooked slowly until the sugar solution thickens. Dehydrated sweet potatoes may be used, in which case they are soaked and then treated as fresh ones.

Fried. Same as recipe for fresh white potatoes.

Baked with Apples. Place a layer of sliced, cooked sweet potatoes in a greased baking pan. Upon it place a layer of sliced fresh or soaked dried apples. Season with salt, pepper and brown sugar. Repeat until the desired amount has been prepared. Pour hot water, that in which potatoes were cooked, and to which has been added a little butter, over the food until it just shows through the top layer. Bake until apples are done.

BEANS, BOILED OR STEWED

Clean the beans, picking out the defective ones and any possible stones. Soak them for several hours or over night, if possible. Boil 4 cups (for four men) for about ½ hour. While the beans are parboiling, parboil separately about 1 pound of salt pork. (If bacon is to be used, it need not be parboiled unless it is very salty.) Skim the beans from time to time as the scum rises. Drain both the beans and pork, place in one kettle and add about 2 qts. of boiling water, and boil slowly until done (about 2 hours). When they are almost done, season with salt and pepper. A small onion or equivalent, diced, may be added when the beans and pork are put together. A tablespoonful of brown sugar and a bit of dry mustard, added with the salt and pepper, gives the beans a good flavor.

FRIED BEANS

Leftover boiled beans may be heated in bacon fat in a frying pan. If no bacon fat is available, a slice or two of bacon may be cut into small pieces and the beans fried in the resulting fat without removing the small pieces of bacon.

BAKED BEANS—USUAL STOVE METHOD

Soak and parboil beans and pork as for stewed beans (see above). Place half the beans in the bottom of the kettle or pot. Then place the salt pork or bacon (in one piece) on those beans and pour the remaining beans over it. Season with salt, pepper, a little onion, 1 tablespoonful of brown sugar or molasses, and a pinch of dry mustard. Be careful not to use too much salt since the pork or bacon is somewhat salty. If the camp larder contains a generous supply of ketchup, a half cup may be added to the beans in place of the sugar. Bake in slow oven 5 to 6 hours.

BEANS BAKED OVER OPEN FIRE

Prepare beans as for oven baking but instead of cooking in oven hang the kettle high over the fire where the beans will not scorch and "bake" about 2 to 3 hours. A very small amount of water must be added from time to time.

BEANS BAKED IN A REFLECTOR

Prepare beans as for baked beans above, but cook them until about ¾ done over the fire. Then pour them into the bake pan which has been greased and finish baking in the reflector. Season as above.

BEANS BAKED IN A HOLE

See notes on page 81.

DRIED BAKED BEANS

Dried baked beans are very convenient to carry on trips when there is not time to cook them in the usual manner. Bake the beans in the usual way and when done pour off whatever liquid there may be. Spread them out thinly in a shallow pan, such as a baking pan, and dry in slow oven or over a slow fire, stirring constantly. When dried, they can be carried in a bag. To prepare them, simply add a little hot water and warm thoroughly. If the weather is very cold, the beans may be frozen instead of dried, stirring them occasionally while they freeze. Prepare for use the same as if they were dried. Frozen cooked beans are carried very often by hunters and trappers in the North.

ROAST BEANS AND CHEESE LOAF

2 cups cooked beans	1½ tsp. salt
2 cups grated cheese	¼ tsp. pepper
	1 cup bread crumbs

Chop beans finely; add cheese, crumbs, and seasoning. Add enough water to form into a stiff roll. Shape and bake, basting occasionally with fat and water. Two or three slices of bacon may be placed over the loaf, thus supplying basting.

BEAN CROQUETTES

2 cups cooked navy or soup beans	4 tbsp. fat
½ cup bread crumbs	½ tsp. Worcestershire sauce (may be omitted)
2 eggs	Salt and pepper

Chop beans finely; add remaining ingredients; shape into form of cutlets or croquettes, roll in crumbs or flour. Fry in hot fat until brown. Serve with medium White Sauce, to which may be added a little horseradish or tomato ketchup.

BOILED OR STEWED LIMA BEANS

Cook as navy or pea beans. See page 159.

CREAMED LIMA BEANS

Soak two cups dried beans over night, cook in boiling salted water until soft; drain, add 1 cup milk or cream, and season with butter, salt and pepper. Reheat before serving.

BAKED LIMA BEANS AND CARROTS

Soak 2 cups dried lima beans, drain, put in baking pan, sprinkle with ½ teaspoon salt and a little pepper. Cut a two-inch cube of fat salt pork or bacon into small pieces.

Fry the meat, add ½ cup sliced fresh carrots or ¼ cup soaked dried carrots and stir constantly until vegetables are browned. Add to beans, dot over with butter, add water to ½ depth of beans. Cover and cook in a slow oven until beans are soft.

LIMA BEANS BAKED WITH BROWN SUGAR AND BACON

When boiled lima beans are half done, pour into a greased baking pan. Sprinkle over them brown sugar (3 tablespoons sugar to 2 cups beans). Season with salt and pepper. Lay slices of bacon over them and bake slowly.

CANNED CORN

Heat 1 can of corn to which has been added a little milk (¼ cup) and a little butter, salt and pepper.

STEWED DRIED CORN

Soak 1½ cups of dried corn if time permits. Otherwise put it on to cook in about 4 cups of cold water. Cook until corn is done, about 45 minutes. Add extra water if necessary. Season with a little salt, pepper, butter, and milk.

STEWED DRIED CORN WITH BACON

Prepare dried corn for stewing as given above. When it is put on to cook add about 8 thin slices of bacon and two or three slices of onion. Cook until bacon is done (when it may be easily cut with a fork), about 45 to 50 minutes.

BAKED DRIED CORN

When stewed corn is about half done, season, and pour into a greased baking pan. Lay a few strips of bacon on top of the corn and bake until corn is done and bacon browned and crisp. A little onion and green pepper may be added to beans, if desired.

CORN FRITTERS

2 cups drained cooked corn	2 tsp. salt
1¼ cup flour	1½ tsp. baking powder
	2 eggs or equiv. in substitute

Chop corn, and add dry ingredients mixed well; beat yolk of eggs until thick and fold in whites beaten stiff (or the equivalent in well-beaten egg powder). Fry in hot fat. Drain on paper before serving.

SUCCOTASH

Combine equal quantities of cooked corn and lima beans; season with butter, salt and pepper. Reheat before serving.

COLD CANNED TOMATOES

Cold, canned tomatoes seasoned well, with salt, pepper, and a little vinegar or lemon juice, if one cares for it, (and if the larder provides) makes a most refreshing "salad."

STEWED TOMATOES

Season a can of tomatoes with butter, salt and pepper, and

a little sugar (1 tablespoon to 2 cups of tomatoes), and a few slices of well-soaked dehydrated onion. Cook until the onion is almost done. Then add slowly a tablespoonful of flour mixed to a thin paste with some of the liquid from the tomatoes. Boil 1 or 2 minutes and serve.

ESCALLOPED TOMATOES

Empty contents of a can of tomatoes into a baking pan, add enough bread, crackers, or hardtack to take up most of the juice. Season with salt, pepper, onion, and sugar, if desired. Lay small slices of bacon on top and bake until bacon is nicely done.

BOILED ONIONS

Put onions of uniform size in cold water and remove skins while under water. Place in pan and cover with boiling salted water; boil gently for 5 minutes, drain and again cover with boiling salted water. Cook until soft but not broken, 10 to 30 minutes. Drain, add a little milk or cream, cook slowly 5 minutes, and season with butter, salt and pepper. Soaked dehydrated onions may be used.

CREAMED ONIONS

Prepare and cook as boiled onions, changing water twice; drain and reheat in medium White Sauce. (See page 147)

FRIED ONIONS

Remove skins from onions; cut in thin slices and put in a

hot frying pan with enough bacon fat to fry them. Dehydrated soaked and drained onions may be used. Cook until brown, stirring frequently. Sprinkle with salt about 1 minute before they are done.

BOILED RICE

1 cup rice	2 qts. boiling water
1 tbsp. salt	

Add rice slowly to boiling salted water, so that the boiling is not checked. Boil 20 minutes, or until rice is done, which may be determined by pressing a grain between the thumb and forefinger. If it mashes easily and completely it is done. Drain and pour over the rice a quart of cold water which is, in turn, drained off. Cover, place high above the fire, and let stand to dry off, when the kernels will be distinct. When stirring rice, always use a fork to avoid breaking kernels, and stir it gently and no more than necessary. Raisins may be added when the rice is almost done.

RICE WITH CHEESE, NO. 1

1 cup rice	2 qts. water
¼ lb. cheese	Butter
1 tbsp. salt	Milk

Boil rice as directed above; cover bottom of greased baking pan with rice, dot with a little butter, and sprinkle with small thin pieces of cheese. Repeat until all the rice and cheese are used. Add milk to half the depth of contents of dish. Bake until cheese melts.

RICE WITH CHEESE, NO. 2

1 cup rice
¼ lb. cheese

½ cup hot milk
2 qts. water
1 tbsp. salt

Boil rice as directed above. After it has dried, add hot milk and cheese which has been cut into small pieces. Reheat until cheese is melted.

FRIED RICE NO. 1

When boiled rice is left over, spread it in a pan or pack in baking powder tins, rinsed in cold water. When ready to use the rice, turn it out, cut in slices and fry in bacon grease. May be served as a vegetable or, with syrup, as a dessert.

FRIED RICE NO. 2

Cut 3 slices of bacon into small pieces and fry. Pour fresh boiled rice (after it has been drained and dried) into the frying pan with the bacon. Fry until the rice is nicely browned. Season well with salt, pepper, and cooked dehydrated onion.

SPANISH RICE

1 cup rice
2 quarts water
1 cup tomatoes

1 onion or equivalent in
  dehydrated onion
Bacon
Salt, pepper

Boil rice as directed above; pour into a greased baking pan, add tomatoes, onion, salt and pepper. Mix thoroughly. Lay a few strips of bacon over the rice and bake until the bacon is nicely browned.

CURRIED RICE

Pour hot curry sauce (see page 148) over freshly boiled rice and serve immediately.

RICE PILAF

3 tbsp. butter (or bacon fat)
2 tbsp. chopped onion
1 cup raw rice

3 cups broth
Salt, pepper
Mushrooms, green pepper, or nuts (optional)

Melt fat in kettle. Add rice and onion. Cook 2–3 minutes, stirring constantly. Add broth, salt and pepper. Simmer 20 minutes or until liquid is absorbed. Add fried mushrooms etc. if desired.

Salads

BEET SALAD WITH SOUR SAUCE

12 small beets
2 tbsp. fat
2 tbsp. flour
Water

¼ cup vinegar
½ cup milk or cream
1 teaspoon sugar
Salt, pepper

Cook the beets, either fresh or dehydrated, in water until tender. Pour off the water in which they were cooked, saving one-half cup of it. If fresh beets are used, cook them without peeling and with root and about 2 inches of stem on. When tender put immediately in cold water and rub off the skins. Reheat the beets in the following sauce.

Sour sauce: Melt the fat and stir in the flour and add beet water. Then add vinegar, milk or cream, sugar, salt and pepper. Cook until slightly thickened.

HARVARD BEETS

12 small cooked beets	2 tbsp. butter
½ tbsp. cornstarch	½ cup sugar
	½ cup vinegar

Slice beets and add to following sauce. Then let them stand in a warm place for one-half hour, add butter and serve.
Sauce: Mix sugar and cornstarch, add one-half cup of vinegar and let boil for 5 minutes, add butter and beets.

SOUR CABBAGE SALAD

1 small head cabbage, shredded	2 tbsp. vinegar
(or equivalent in dehydrated)	½ tsp. salt
2 tbsp. butter or bacon fat,	½ tbsp. sugar
or 2 slices of bacon	Pepper

Cut bacon into small pieces and fry until lightly browned. If butter or bacon fat is used instead melt them. Add cabbage, salt and pepper. Cover and cook until the cabbage is tender. Add vinegar and sugar; cook 5 minutes more.

BEAN-CABBAGE SALAD

2 cups cooked beans	Vinegar
2 cups cooked cabbage	Salt, pepper
1 onion	Sugar (if needed)
Pickle	Mustard (dry)

Mix beans with cabbage. Add finely chopped onion and pickle. Season to taste with salt, pepper, sugar (very small amount needed), mustard, and vinegar. Other cooked vegetables may be added to salad. Also small bits of cooked meat may be used.

GREENS

Early in the season there are frequently available a variety of young wild plants which make excellent substitutes for spinach. The most common and most widely known are dandelion, lamb's quarter, wild mustard, and watercress.

FRESH GREEN SALAD

Wash greens in cold water (add a little salt if the greens are sandy or very dirty). Only tender leaves and young stems should be used. Season with salt, pepper, and vinegar.

WILTED GREENS

Cut a few slices of bacon in small pieces. Fry, when done add a little vinegar (if strong dilute with half water), pepper, salt, 1 tablespoon of flour, and a little sugar. While boiling-hot pour this sauce over greens which have been washed and chopped into small pieces.

BOILED GREENS

Wash greens thoroughly, removing roots and tough stems. Cook until tender, about 30 minutes for dandelions, in boiling salted water. Season with butter, or bacon fat, salt and pepper. Serve plain or with vinegar. A few strips of bacon or a small piece of salt pork may be cooked with the greens.

BOILED SALAD DRESSING

¼ tablespoon salt	2 tablespoons flour
1 tsp. mustard	1 egg (or equivalent in
1½ tbsp. sugar	dehydrated)
¾ cup milk	1½ tbsp. melted fat
	¼ cup vinegar

Mix dry ingredients, add egg slightly beaten, fat, milk, and vinegar very slowly. Cook over boiling water until mixture thickens. This dressing may be used with almost any assortment of vegetables, meat, and fish to make a good camp salad.

EAGLE BRAND MAGIC MAYONNAISE

⅔ cup Eagle Brand sweet-ened condensed milk	1 egg yolk (or equivalent)
¼ cup vinegar or lemon juice	½ teaspoon salt
	1 teaspoon dry mustard
¼ cup salad oil or melted butter	Few grains cayenne

Place ingredients in mixing bowl. Beat with rotary egg beater until mixture thickens. If thicker consistency is desired place in cool place to chill before serving. Makes 1¼ cups.

Chapter Nine
DESSERTS, JELLIES, JAMS, AND BEVERAGES

DRIED FRUITS—STEWED

One of the best camp desserts is properly cooked dehydrated fruit. It is not only pleasing to the taste but also a very important part of the camp diet. Much of the prejudice against dehydrated fruits can be traced directly to improper cooking.

Most dehydrated fruit, unless one is instructed otherwise by directions on the package, is improved by soaking from 12 to 24 hours in enough cold water to just cover. Spices, such as stick cinnamon or a few cloves may be added if desired. To stew, simmer or boil the fruit gently in the water in which it is soaked, until tender. This usually requires from 20 to 30 minutes. Most prunes need no sugar and other fruits need very little.

FRUIT COBBLER

½ cup shortening
2 cups flour
2 tsp. baking powder
Salt

Fruit—fresh, canned, dehydrated
Sugar
½ cup milk (or half milk and half water)

Cut shortening into mixed flour, baking powder, salt. Add milk slowly. Put dough on floured "board" and pat out to shape of pan. Place fruit and sugar with juice to half cover fruit in greased baking pan. Place dough over fruit. Cut a few holes in dough so steam may escape. Bake in hot oven for 30–40 minutes. Serve with milk or cream.

APPLE DUMPLINGS NO. 1

Make a biscuit dough and roll thin, about ¼ inch thick. Peel and quarter some apples, one for each dumpling, or use ¼ cup of previously cooked dehydrated apples for each dumpling. Lay each portion of apples on a piece of dough large enough to completely cover the apple when the edges are drawn together. Sprinkle the apple with a little sugar and cinnamon and cover with the dough, pinching the dampened (with water) edges together. Place in a greased reflector pan and pour around them the following sauce. Serve with milk or milk slightly seasoned with sugar and cinnamon.

4 tbsp. sugar	1 cup water
2 tbsp. cornstarch	1 tbsp. butter

Mix sugar and cornstarch, add water, boil for two minutes; add butter. Then pour around dumplings in pans.

APPLE DUMPLINGS No. 2

Pastry dough may be used instead of biscuit dough with excellent results. Make pastry according to one of the recipes below. Roll thin. Lay each portion of apples on a piece of dough large enough to completely cover the apples when the edges are drawn together. Sprinkle apples with a little sugar, cinnamon and butter (if available), cover with the dough,

— 173 —

pinching the dampened edges together. Place in a pan and bake 30 minutes in a very hot oven. Serve with milk or cream.

COLD WATER PIE CRUST

3 cups flour	¼ tsp. salt
1 cup shortening (cold)	10 tbsp. cold water

Best results are obtained by having all ingredients and utensils as cold as possible. Cut shortening into flour and salt with two knives until mixture looks like meal or until fat is in pieces about the size of a pea. Hold knives, one in each hand, crossing the blades. Then pull the hands away from each other. Repeat. Add cold water a little at a time, mixing with a knife until the dough cleans the bowl of all flour. *Avoid using too much water.* Divide the dough into two parts. Roll each out—one for the upper crust and one for the lower. Lower crust should be slightly larger.

HOT WATER PIE CRUST

1 cup shortening (slightly softened)	½ cup boiling water
3 cups flour (approximately)	½ tsp. baking powder (optional)
	Salt

Place shortening in a bowl or pan and pour the boiling water over it. Add salt, then flour and baking powder until no more can be stirred in. Divide the dough in two pieces, one for upper and one for lower crust. Roll dough into thin sheets. This amount of dough makes a double crusted pie for a reflector pan 18 by 7 inches.

FRUIT PIE

Line a pie pan with a crust made by one of recipes above.
Sprinkle it with 4 tbsp. flour and 2 tbsp. sugar. Pour into this
the fruit, enough to fill the pan (a reflector pan 18 by 7 inches
takes 1½ to 2 lbs. of dried apricots or peaches). If dried
fruit is used, it must be previously cooked; fresh fruit need
not be. Sprinkle a little flour (about 2 tbsp.) and a little sugar
(about 2 tbsp.) over the fruit. Moisten the upper edges of the
lower crust. Place over it the upper crust, which has had a
few small holes made in it either in the form of a design or
just holes. Press the two edges together tightly, trim off any
extra dough. Crimp the edges between thumb and fingers
so that the juice may not escape. Bake in moderately hot
heat at 450° for 15 minutes and then at 350° for 30 to 40
minutes.

DEEP FRUIT PIE

Place well-seasoned fruit in a deep pan, moisten edges of pan,
and cover with a crust. Bake in moderate heat until crust is
nicely browned.

CHOCOLATE PIE

2 tbsp. Crisco	2 egg yolks (if available)
6 tbsp. flour	1 tsp. vanilla
1½ cup milk	2 tbsp. granulated sugar
2 sq. unsweetened chocolate	(if available)
¾ cup sugar	2 egg whites (if available)
¼ tsp. salt	Baked pie shell

Melt Crisco. Add chocolate and keep over low fire until chocolate is melted (stirring constantly). Add flour, sugar, salt, milk. Bring slowly to boil, stirring constantly until thick and smooth. Remove from fire and add egg yolk. If eggs are a-vailable, make a meringue by whipping 2 whites until stiff, add 2 tbsp. sugar. Place meringue on top of pie and brown in moderate heat.

TARTS OR TURNOVERS

Roll pastry dough ¼ inch thick; cut into 3-inch squares. Place jelly or jam on one half. Fold other half over it and press the edges tightly together after the lower edge has been moistened. Make a few small holes in the upper crust and bake as fruit pie.

COTTAGE PUDDING

¼ to ½ cup butter or any shortening	1 egg or substitute
1 cup sugar	2 tsp. baking powder
2 cups flour	¼ tsp. salt
1 cup milk	1 tsp. vanilla (if available)

Cream shortening and sugar; add flour, to which baking powder and salt have been added, alternately with the milk. Beat well. Pour the batter into a pan which has been greased and dusted with flour. Bake at a moderate temperature for about 30 minutes or until the cake rises up again after being pressed gently with a finger, and until the edges have drawn away from the sides of the pan.

1 cup of raisins, dates, or nuts may be added to the batter. 1 tsp. of cinnamon also does well for flavoring. Five tbsp. of

cocoa or 2 oz. (2 small squares) of bitter chocolate may be added to the batter and a good chocolate pudding result. Twice this recipe will fill a reflector pan 7 in. × 18 in. Lemon or Chocolate Sauce (see page 183) or stewed fruit may be served with the pudding.

APPLESAUCE CAKE

½ cup shortening
1 cup sugar
1¾ cups flour
1 tsp. soda
¼ tsp. salt
1 tsp. cinnamon
½ tsp. cloves (if available)

1 egg beaten light (or equiv.)
1 cup raisins, cut fine and floured
1 cup nuts (if available) cut fine, floured
1 cup thick applesauce

Cream shortening and sugar. Add egg, raisins, nuts, soda, salt, spices, and flour to creamed mixture, alternately with applesauce, a small amount at a time. Beat after each addition until smooth. Bake in moderate heat about 1 hour. This is also an excellent camp cake.

PRUNE CAKE

1½ cups prunes
¾ cup sugar
½ cup prune juice
1¾ cups flour

½ cup shortening
1 egg (or substitute)
1 tsp. soda
Salt

Cook prunes, and combine in order of prunes, shortening, sugar, egg, prune juice, soda, and flour. Bake as cottage pudding. This is an excellent camp cake.

CHOCOLATE CAKE

1 cup shortening
1 cup sugar
2 squares cooking chocolate
3 cups flour
1 cup milk

½ cup nuts (optional)
3 eggs (or substitutes) well beaten
5 tsp. baking powder
1 tsp. vanilla (optional)

Mix and bake as cottage pudding.

HERMITS

⅓ cup shortening
⅔ cup sugar
1 egg (or substitute)
2 tbsp. milk

1¾ cups flour
2 tsp. baking powder
⅓ cup raisins (cut fine)
1 tsp. cinnamon

Cream butter and sugar, add raisins, egg (well beaten), and milk. Mix dry ingredients and add to first mixture. Roll thin, cut, and bake in a hot oven.

OATMEAL COOKIES

½ cup shortening
1 cup sugar
1 egg
5 tbsp. milk
1¾ cups rolled oats

½ cup raisins
½ cup nuts (if available)
1½ cups flour
½ tsp. salt
½ tsp. soda
1 tsp. cinnamon

Cream shortening and sugar; then add egg (well beaten), milk, rolled oats, raisins, and nuts. Mix flour with remaining ingredients and add to first mixture. Drop from a spoon on a greased pan and bake in a moderate heat 15–20 minutes.

RICH COOKIES

½ cup butter
⅓ cup sugar
1 egg (well beaten) or
   substitute

Raisins
¾ cup flour
½ tsp. vanilla (if avail-
   able)

Cream butter and sugar. Add egg, flour, and vanilla. Drop from tip of spoon on greased pan two inches apart. Spread thinly with a knife first dipped in cold water. Place raisin in center of each cookie, sprinkle with sugar and bake for 15 minutes in moderate heat.

DOUGHNUTS

2 cups flour
½ tsp. salt
2 tsp. baking powder

½ cup sugar
½ cup milk
1 egg (or substitute) well
   beaten

Make a batter and beat thoroughly. Roll to about ½ inch thickness. Cut into rings or strips which may be twisted. Fry in very hot fat until nicely browned, turning when one side is browned. Drain and roll in sugar if desired.

RICE PUDDING

2 cups boiled rice
4 cups milk
Sugar to taste

Cinnamon
½ cup raisins
2 eggs or substitute
Salt

Mix rice, milk, sugar, salt, eggs well beaten, and raisins. Pour into a greased pan. Sprinkle with cinnamon and bake one hour. Serve with milk.

BLUEBERRY PUDDING

¾ cup sugar   ½ tsp. salt
¼ cup shortening   ¾ cup milk
2 cups flour   1 egg or substitute
3 tsp. baking powder   2 cups blueberries

Mix as for cake, stir in floured berries last, and bake in moderate heat. Serve with creamy sauce (page 183). Other fruit may be used in place of blueberries.

BREAD PUDDING

4 cups old bread   1 tbsp. butter
4 cups milk   ½ cup suagr
2 eggs (or equivalent)   Vanilla (if available)
                                Salt

Heat milk and add butter, sugar, and bread broken into small pieces. Let stand 20 minutes, then add eggs (beaten if fresh) vanilla and salt. Pour into a greased pan and place the pan in a larger pan of hot water. Bake about one hour or until the pudding does not adhere to a knife blade inserted to the center of the pudding. Serve hot with hard sauce or cold with milk or other sauces (page 183).

Fruit Bread Pudding. Add ⅓ cup cooked fruit, jam, marmalade, or raisins to the pudding before baking. The sugar may need to be increased for some fruits.

Chocolate Bread Pudding. To the basic recipe add 1 ounce of baking chocolate or ¼ cup of cocoa (mixed with the sugar). Increase the sugar in the original recipe to 1 cup. This is a real party dessert if served hot with hard sauce.

CORNSTARCH PUDDING

3 tbsp. sugar	⅛ tsp. salt
3 tbsp. cornstarch	2 cups milk (scald if fresh)
	Vanilla (if available)

Mix sugar, salt, and cornstarch; stir while adding milk slowly. Bring to boil, then place pan in larger pan of hot water (improvised double boiler) and cook slowly for 25 minutes, stirring occasionally. Add vanilla and pour into pan or cups to cool. Serve with milk.

CHOCOLATE CORNSTARCH PUDDING

Use above recipe but increase sugar to 5 or 6 tbsp. Add 1 ½ squares (1½ oz.) of melted chocolate. Then proceed as in above recipe.

INDIAN PUDDING

⅓ cup cornmeal	¼ tsp. cinnamon
Salt	3 cups milk
½ tsp. ginger	⅓ cup molasses (or brown sugar)

Mix dry ingredients, add milk and molasses or sugar, cook slowly for 15–20 minutes. Pour into a greased pan and bake in a slow oven for 2–2½ hours. Stir occasionally the first half hour. Serve hot with milk or, if the larder can afford it—hard sauce.

A rather good pudding can be made by cooking the ingredients, without baking, over a low fire. The pudding would have to be watched closely and stirred frequently to keep it from burning.

FRUIT PUDDING

Stew enough dried or fresh fruit to make the required number of servings. When the fruit is about half cooked, sweeten to taste. Place small biscuits on top of the fruit. (See page 96 for recipe.) Cover quickly and boil 15 minutes. *Do not remove cover while biscuits are cooking* or they will be soggy!

EAGLE BRAND CARAMEL PUDDING

Boil a can of Eagle or Reindeer milk (in unopened can) slowly for four hours. Chill thoroughly and serve with whipped cream.

WHIPPED CREAM

Fairly successful whipped cream can be had in camp from Evaporated or Powdered milk, and is a splendid surprise. One of the following sets of directions should be followed very carefully.

WHIPPED EVAPORATED MILK NO. 1
Heat undiluted evaporated milk over water 10 minutes. Chill *very* thoroughly. Keep the milk very cold (in a pan of cold mountain stream or spring water). Beat with a fork or preferably egg beater.

WHIPPED EVAPORATED MILK NO. 2
Beat the milk (just as it comes from can) for several minutes. Add juice of half a lemon slowly, beating all the while until milk thickens. If necessary add a little more lemon juice and continue beating.

WHIPPED POWDERED MILK

Measure 6 tablespoons of cold water into a pan, add 4½ tablespoons powdered milk, and beat until smooth. Place over hot water and cook three minutes. Chill very thoroughly and whip, keeping it very cold.

Sauces

FRUIT SAUCE

Cook any fresh fruit until done. Sweeten, and cook until it thickens slightly. Pour over pudding. Canned fruit may be used instead of fresh. Spices may be added to sauce if desired.

CREAMY SAUCE

¼ cup butter (do not use lard or bacon fat)
½ cup sugar

½ cup cream or undiluted evaporated milk
1 tsp. vanilla

Cream butter and sugar, add cream slowly. Beat well and just before serving place over hot water and stir until smooth and creamy. Add vanilla and serve. (Do not melt butter.)

CHOCOLATE SAUCE

1 cup sugar
4 tbsp. cocoa
1 tbsp. flour

½ cup milk
1 tsp. vanilla
⅛ tsp. salt
1 tbsp. butter

Mix dry ingredients, add milk, stirring constantly. Boil 2 minutes, add vanilla, salt, and butter.

HARD SAUCE

¼ cup butter
¾ cup sugar
1 tbsp. hot water (rum or
  brandy is better)

Vanilla (omit if rum or
  brandy is used)

Cream butter, add sugar slowly. Add vanilla and hot water
a few drops at a time, continuing to cream the mixture. When
the mixture is well creamed, serve on a hot pudding.

LEMON SAUCE

1 egg (or 1 tsp. cornstarch)
1 cup sugar
¼ cup butter

1 tsp. grated lemon rind
  (optional)
3 tbsp. lemon juice
½ cup water

Beat egg slightly. Add other ingredients and cook until thickened and smooth, stirring constantly. If cornstarch is used
instead of egg, mix it with the sugar.

Jellies and Jams

FRUIT JELLY

Any tart fresh fruit such as apples or berries may be used.
Boil one pound of fruit until it is very done. Strain off juice
(preferably through cheesecloth). Add as much sugar to
juice as there is juice. Boil again until juice is quite thick.
Pour into molds and cool.

JAM

Jams, and very good ones, too, may be made from dried fruit. Cook the fruit in a very small amount of water until it is done, mash, and add three-fourths as much sugar as fruit. Cook again until the jam is thickened.

APPLESAUCE

Stew dried apples until they are soft. Mash, sweeten to taste and cook until slightly thickened. Sprinkle with cinnamon and serve.

Beverages

COFFEE

Heat water until it is boiling rapidly. Add 1 tbsp. of coffee for each cup of water. Let it come to a boil three times, removing it from the fire for a second after each time. After the third time, remove from fire, settle grounds, with 1 tbsp. of cold water poured in very gently.

TEA

Bring the desired amount of water to a hard boil (in an open kettle), then add ½ tsp. tea for each cup of water (amount depends upon brand of tea and strength desired). Remove from fire immediately, stir to settle leaves, cover, and steep for four minutes. Pour liquid from leaves immediately and it is ready to serve.

CHOCOLATE

1 cup water
1 cup milk
1 oz. or square chocolate
  (bitter cooking chocolate)

Pinch of salt
Sugar to taste

Heat milk and water to boiling point, add chocolate, finely cut, and sugar. Stir until sugar and chocolate are dissolved.

COCOA

4 cups milk
1½ tbsp. cocoa

2 tbsp. sugar
½ cup hot water

Scald milk (if fresh milk is used). Mix cocoa and sugar, add hot water and boil 3 minutes. Add milk and reheat.

List of
BOOKS ON CAMPING

BATES, JOSEPH D., *Outdoor Cook's Bible*, Doubleday, 1964.

Family Camping Directory, Barcom, Inglewood, California.

KEPHART, HORACE, *Camping and Woodcraft*, 2 volumes in 1, MacMillan, 1948.

MABEE, SOURDOUGH JACK, *Sourdough Jack's Western Cookbook*. Box 4091, San Francisco, California, 1959

NESSMUK, *Woodcraft*, Dover, 1963

WELLS, GEORGE AND IRIS, *The Handbook of Wilderness Travel*, Harper, 1956.

List of
CAMP OUTFITTERS
FOOD PROCESSORS AND SUPPLIERS

California—Lynwood
  Dri-lite Foods, 11333 Atlantic, 90261
California—San Francisco
  Abercrombie and Fitch C., 220 Post Street, 94108
California—San José
  Bernard Foods, 222 South 24th Street, 95103
Colorado—Boulder
  Gerry's, 80301
Illinois—Chicago
  Bernard Foods, 217 Jefferson Street, 60606
Illinois—Elk Grove Village
  Seidel's Trail Packet Food, 70007
Maine—Freeport
  L. L. Bean, 04032
Massachusetts—Cohasset
  Stow-a-way Products, Dept. U.F., 103 Ripley Road, 02025
Minnesota—St. Paul
  Gokey's, 94 East 4th Street, 55101
New Jersey—Somerville
  Raemco Inc., P. O. Box 482
New York—New York
  Camp and Trail Outfitters, 112 Chambers Street, 1007
  Abercrombie and Fitch C., Madison Avenue at 45th
    Street, 10017

Texas—New Braunfels
   New Braunfels Smokehouse, P. O. Box 1159
Washington—Seattle
   Eddie Bauer, 98122
Wyoming—Jackson Hole
   Norm Thompson, Outfitters, 83001
Canada
   Bernard Foods, 120 Sunrise Avenue, Toronto, Ontario
   Timothy Eaton Co., St. Catharine's Street, Montreal,
   Quebec

INDEX

TUTTLE COOKBOOKS

Brazilian Cookery, *by Margarette de Andrade*
California Mission Recipes, *by Bess A. Cleveland*
Campers' Cookbook, *by Lucy G. Raup*
Court Dishes of China, *by Lucille Davis*
Dining in Spain, *by Gerrie Beene and Lourdes King*
Early American Beverages, *by John Hull Brown*
Early American Herb Recipes, *by Alice Cooke Brown*
French-Canadian Cookbook, *by E. Donald Asselin*
German-American Cookery, *by Brigitte S. Simms*
Japanese Cuisine: A Culinary Tour, *by John D. Keys*
Low Carbohydrate Cookery, *by Dolly and Jack Schumann*
Pineapples, Passion Fruit and Poi, *by Mary Lou Gebhard*
Portuguese-American Cookbook, *by E. Donald Asselin*
Specialty Cuts and How to Cook Them, *by Kate Sherry*
What's Cooking on Okinawa, *by Kubasaki High School*

edited, designed, or produced by
ROLAND A. MULHAUSER

OTHER TUTTLE COOKBOOKS

Art of Chinese Cooking, *by Benedictine Sisters of Peking*
Art of Korean Cooking, *by Harriet Morris*
Chinese Cooking Made Easy, *by Rosy Tseng*
Chow: Secrets of Chinese Cooking, *by Dolly Chow*
Dining with Celebrities, *by Selma Cherkas*
Hawaiian Cuisine, *by Hawaiian Society of Washington, D.C.*
Hors D'Oeuvres, Embassy Recipes, *by Shom Edmond*
In a Persian Kitchen, *by Naideh Mazda*
Let's Make Candy, *by Noy Alexander*
Mrs. Ma's Chinese Cookbook, *by Nancy Chih Ma*
Recipes from the East, *by Irma Walker Ross*
Rice and Spice, *by Phyllis Jervey*
Siamese Cookery, *by Marie M. Wilson*
World of Parties, *by Phyllis Jervey*